Influences and Inspirations in Curriculum Studies Research and Teaching

This volume highlights lived experiences, personal inspirations and motivations, which have generated scholarship, and influenced the research and teaching of scholars in the field of curriculum studies.

Offering contributions from new, established and experienced scholars, chapters foreground the ways in which the authors have been influenced by the mentorship and work of others, by personal challenges, and by the contexts in which they live and work. Chapters also illustrate how scholars have engaged in a variety of methodological and autobiographical processes including narrative and poetic inquiry, autoethnography and visual arts research. Through a range of contributions, the book clarifies the origins and legacy of contemporary curriculum studies and in doing so, provides inspiration for beginning scholars and academics as they continue to find their voices in academic communities.

Offering rich insight into the experiences and scholarship of a wide range of scholars, this volume will be of interest to students, scholars and researchers with an interest in curriculum studies, as well as educational research and methodologies more broadly.

Carmen Shields is Professor Emerita in the Schulich School of Education, Nipissing University, Canada.

Adam Garry Podolski completed his PhD in Educational Sustainability at Nipissing University, Canada.

John J. Guiney Yallop is Professor in the School of Education, Faculty of Professional Studies, Acadia University, Canada.

Studies in Curriculum Theory Series
Series Editor: William F. Pinar, University of British Columbia, Canada

In this age of multimedia information overload, scholars and students may not be able to keep up with the proliferation of different topical, trendy book series in the field of curriculum theory. It will be a relief to know that one publisher offers a balanced, solid, forward-looking series devoted to significant and enduring scholarship, as opposed to a narrow range of topics or a single approach or point of view. This series is conceived as the series busy scholars and students can trust and depend on to deliver important scholarship in the various "discourses" that comprise the increasingly complex field of curriculum theory.

The range of the series is both broad (all of curriculum theory) and limited (only important, lasting scholarship) – including but not confined to historical, philosophical, critical, multicultural, feminist, comparative, international, aesthetic and spiritual topics and approaches. Books in this series are intended for scholars and for students at the doctoral and, in some cases, master's levels.

Theorizing Shadow Education and Academic Success in East Asia
Understanding the Meaning, Value, and Use of Shadow Education by East Asian Students
Young Chun Kim & Jung-Hoon Jung

Curriculum, Environment, and the Work of C. A. Bowers
Ecological and Cultural Perspectives
Edited by Audrey M. Dentith, David Flinders, John Lupinacci, and Jennifer S. Thom

Influences and Inspirations in Curriculum Studies Research and Teaching
Reflections on the Origins and Legacy of Contemporary Scholarship
Edited by Carmen Shields, Adam Garry Podolski, and John J. Guiney Yallop

For more information about this series, please visit: https://www.routledge.com/Studies-in-Curriculum-Theory-Series/book-series/LEASCTS

Influences and Inspirations in Curriculum Studies Research and Teaching
Reflections on the Origins and Legacy of Contemporary Scholarship

Edited by Carmen Shields, Adam Garry Podolski, and John J. Guiney Yallop

NEW YORK AND LONDON

First published 2022
by Routledge
605 Third Avenue, New York, NY 10158

and by Routledge
2 Park Square, Milton Park, Abingdon, Oxon, OX14 4RN

Routledge is an imprint of the Taylor & Francis Group, an informa business

© 2022 selection and editorial matter, Carmen Shields, Adam Garry Podolski, and John J. Guiney Yallop; individual chapters, the contributors

The right of Carmen Shields, Adam Garry Podolski, and John J. Guiney Yallop to be identified as the authors of the editorial material, and of the authors for their individual chapters, has been asserted in accordance with sections 77 and 78 of the Copyright, Designs and Patents Act 1988.

All rights reserved. No part of this book may be reprinted or reproduced or utilised in any form or by any electronic, mechanical, or other means, now known or hereafter invented, including photocopying and recording, or in any information storage or retrieval system, without permission in writing from the publishers.

Trademark notice: Product or corporate names may be trademarks or registered trademarks, and are used only for identification and explanation without intent to infringe.

Library of Congress Cataloging-in-Publication Data
A catalog record for this title has been requested

ISBN: 978-0-367-72264-7 (hbk)
ISBN: 978-0-367-72266-1 (pbk)
ISBN: 978-1-003-15411-2 (ebk)

DOI: 10.4324/9781003154112

Typeset in Sabon
by KnowledgeWorks Global Ltd.

We dedicate this book to all those scholars mentioned by the chapter authors as guides, mentors, inspirations, supporters who have helped us on our journeys.

Contents

Acknowledgements	ix
Gifts, Grace and Gratitude: An Introduction	1
1 I am Grateful for Every Invitation JOHN J. GUINEY YALLOP	22
2 Worlding Gifts, Grace and Gratitude: A Posthuman Pedagogy of Art, Affect and Belonging FIONA BLAIKIE	26
3 The Way of Gratitude ASHWANI KUMAR	37
4 When Curriculum Disrupts: A Case for Gratitude After Decades of Being Surprised CARMEN SCHLAMB	45
5 Serendipity TERESA STRONG-WILSON	52
6 The Labyrinth of Gratitude: A Collage of Memories, Reflections and Gifts in Learning and Teaching MARNI J. BINDER	57
7 Opening to Grace: Curricular Knowing as Spiritual Praxis SARAH MACKENZIE-DAWSON	69
8 Pedagogical Resonances: A Curriculum of Care WALTER GERSHON	77

viii   *Contents*

9   The Butterfly Catcher   83
KATHRYN RICKETTS

10 Aporias: Geo-metrons Sounding in the Silence of the Void   92
PATRICIA PALULIS

11 Dear Carl: A Letter of Gratitude for the Gifts of Education   98
GRAHAM W. LEA

12 Love in the Time of Covid-19: Contemplating the Gifts,
Grace and Gratitude of Carl Leggo as Living with
Intellectual Passion   105
ANITA SINNER

13 The Magic Time: Indigenous Influences on Pedagogies
Linking the Past with the Future   110
JEAN-PAUL RESTOULE

14 A Curriculum Journey Inspired by Picturebooks   116
TARA-LYNN SCHEFFEL

15 (Re)membering Indigenous Curriculum Theorists:
Gifts and Gratitude   123
ADRIAN M. DOWNEY

16 On My Knees: Embracing Adoption to Understand Curriculum   130
DOROTHY VAANDERING

17 Gratitude, Living, and Left Together …   134
ROBERT NELLIS

18 Coming into Being, Again and Again and Again   140
AVRIL AITKEN

19 From a Steel Town Down: Gifts, Grace and Gratitude   147
ADAM GARRY PODOLSKI

20 Revisiting Place: The Gift of Lingering in a Curricular Legacy   154
CARMEN SHIELDS

Index   160

Acknowledgements

We acknowledge, first of all, the authors who contributed their wonderful chapters that make up this book. The writing and images they offer here provide inspiration for us and for others to carry on the legacies they share. We want to acknowledge Bill Pinar who, from the time we first mentioned our proposal to him, warmly welcomed this book to the Routledge Studies in Curriculum Theory Series. Our thanks to the people at Routledge, in particular Elsbeth Wright, AnnaMary Goodall and Katherine Tsamparlis, and a very special thanks to our project manager, Preksha Sharma; a pleasure to work with from the start, they have patiently guided us through the process from proposal to this book. Our life partners have supported us through this project. We are grateful for their unwavering love and care. We also want to acknowledge each other. While we had a deep respect for each other and the work each of us previously created, that respect deepened as we worked together on this book. With trust, patience, generosity and open hearts, we strove to contribute our best and invite the best from each other. We feel we succeeded; this book is the proof. Finally, we thank the readers of this book. Each reader receives the legacies shared and offered in each chapter of this book. Every reader is invited to take those legacies forward so that the space we call Curriculum Studies will always be one of gifts, grace and gratitude.

Gifts, Grace and Gratitude: An Introduction

When we three came together to think about gratitude in our lives as scholars, our conversation turned to the importance of recognizing and acknowledging what has and who have inspired, influenced and guided us in our curriculum journeys. This book emerged from that conversation. Our intention in compiling this text is to provide an opening – an opening to speak about people, places and events that have influenced us profoundly as scholars; collectively, we so rarely seem to share the roots of our beliefs about learning or how we came to them. This book is a place to ponder how we have come to our present-day practice as teachers and researchers, to pay homage to our past experiences, and to honour the people, events and situations we encountered along our learning paths. We invited scholars to join us in writing about what they believe were the gifts from their inspirations and influences and how they are using those gifts in their present life and work. This book then, is a collection of reflections by curriculum studies scholars on the inspirations and influences that guide our teaching and research practices.

The connection between legacy and learning encompasses reflections on situations and events lived with family, with mentors, with teachers and others across time. In those relationships lie passion, joy, hope, sadness, loss – and all else that links us to profound life moments that influence our choices and direction in life and in our scholarly work.

Introduction to the Editors and the Text

The pages of this book are full of stories that offer examples of legacies and the gifts and grace inherent in them. In this section, we weave together our reflections on our own received legacies and the gifts in them that continue to provide the foundation of our thinking and being as curriculum scholars.

DOI: 10.4324/9781003154112-1

2 Introduction

Carmen

For me, this book had its beginning as a doctoral defence came to an end in December 2018. The conversation around the real and virtual table was deep and meaningful. Before we left the room, as Supervisor, I took the opportunity to offer thanks to the committee by turning to each one to remind them of how long we had known one another and where we had met in years gone by. On the virtual screens were committee members John Guiney Yallop, Fiona Blaikie and External Examiner David Booth. In the room was committee member Kathy Mantas and Internal Examiner Heather Rintoul. Since then, both David and Heather have passed away. John is a co-editor of this book, while Fiona has contributed a chapter.

I kept that day in my mind's eye as this book project developed beginning in the spring of 2019. I felt there was grace in that room that day as gifts of connection were mentioned through individuals knowing one another over the years in academic circles, and through the curricular disciplines of poetry, narrative and art. From that day I carry a legacy of friendship with those named above, and the knowledge of what can be accomplished when colleagues are called upon to give their experience to a new member of the academy. I found it a very moving day.

Ashwani Kumar, among other authors in the pages that follow, has commented on the fact that as academics we do not often enough pause to think about and name gifts we have been given or legacies of learning we carry forward with us in our teaching and research. I feel there is a strong sense of gratitude in the chapters that follow – gratitude for people, for ideas, for places – for gifts given in the course of learning with no expectation of return in the giving. Carmen Schlamb has referred to these gifts as surprises in her chapter – learning as opening unexpected gifts, while Teresa Strong-Wilson has used the word "serendipity" as she shares insights that have affected her vision of curriculum across time. Perhaps like the Prodigal Son, the experience of returning to be greeted by unexpected joy is part of the legacies of learning waiting to be read in this book – returning to think again about the ways we were welcomed by others ready to receive us.

Adam

As a Student Success Teacher working with students labelled as at risk, I find I am often travelling a curriculum of the corridor, a corridor regularly winding its way into unfamiliar passages becoming the type of Labyrinth Marni Binder describes in her chapter, as I encounter the community and voices found in the hallways between classes. Pinar (2011) describes curriculum as a complicated conversation. I too, in my Student Success role, experience curriculum in this way; it can be very

Introduction 3

complicated – at times even requiring a translation, as life experiences can differ so widely, but in the tension, passion, conflict, presence, love, commitment, vulnerability and release – in the space between, that Ted Aoki (2005) so wisely urged educators to listen to – is a place where I've witnessed learning translate into community. Whether the space is between classes or experiences, it is where I want to be, where I've experienced gifts, grace and gratitude.

By learning with students, from our teachers, people become a part of us – our teachers and their gifts are conjured through us in our responses to others, to help, to heal, to be a part of. Like with genes, there is intercourse that passes on lessons learned, that gives birth to who we are – epistemologically and educationally as teachers – because gifts, grace and gratitude provide a foundation for curriculum theory.

John

From the spring of 2019 to the spring of 2020 when the chapter descriptions, or in some cases full chapters, began to arrive in our inboxes, Carmen, Adam and I had many conversations about how to structure this book, what to offer as a title for it, whom to invite. Those conversations guided us as we listened to or read each other's words. We saw these conversations, and the connections we had with each other and with other academics as, what Sarah MacKenzie-Dawson calls in her chapter, "opportunities to listen deeply." Listening is a gift, both for the listener and for the one being heard. This book is a gift. Each of the chapters and the foreword, this introduction, all are gifts. All are also expressions of gratitude for legacies received while also creations that can become part of those legacies of learning we bring forward.

Carmen

Recently, I received my final promotion, becoming Professor Emerita at Nipissing University. What this last step in a long university career means is that I have many years of teaching, research and service to look back upon. Like Adam, I was once a support teacher, called a Resource Teacher, in a Nova Scotia school system. My focus for eight years was working with students with learning disabilities as they struggled to understand words, school requirements, relationships and, in some cases, their lives. The gifts I received in that learning ground have held me through my years teaching courses in three universities where, in each place, I found graduate students struggling to learn about school teaching, relationships, their students' lives, and their own lives.

Thanks to my doctoral supervisor, Mick Connelly, I learned that each of us has life experience that is a more profound teacher than any schoolwork could be. My job became one of helping graduate students

4 *Introduction*

translate their lived reality into their personal and professional lives, most often using my experience as a tangible example. Bill Pinar (1994) has called this move "teaching from within."

I now have more than 25 years of gathering shared stories of experience from around both real and virtual graduate tables to count as gifts given and received. They are now stories remembered in my heart and soul. Perhaps most especially, the grace I have experienced working individually with those who chose to complete their graduate work with me has been humbling, exhilarating and life changing. I carry with me a legacy provided by their willingness to open doors for learning through which neither they, nor I, knew what would unfold. New ways of living in the world have been revealed in our exchanges and I have been privileged to walk into worlds I might otherwise never have known.

Adam

As an academic, although I haven't travelled the distance John and Carmen have, there have been several big moments for me already. One was at my Doctoral Defence. David Booth was on my Committee. I asked Carmen what type of person he was; she said he was the type of person that opens up a path for others – Carmen's response, and her description of David, and David himself, offer the type of grace, gifts and gratitude that are found in this book. David reminded me at the end of my defence that a successful narrative study begins when "I know I'm the tale." Another big moment, or curriculum encounter, occurred for me in Montreal, Quebec, at McGill University where I met Carl Leggo at the Provoking Curriculum Conference. I experienced Carl Leggo as a *presence*, as a *spirit*, as much as a person. Professor Leggo was reflecting on his learning with Ted Aoki, composing poetry from Ted's work and words – I could sense the intimate connection between Carl and Ted as Carl translated Ted's words into poetry. The experience was a gift, magical even, in its expression of gratitude and love, or is it grace when one exceptional scholar honours another? I feel Carl's presence; experience his legacy again when I read the chapters written by Graham Lea, Robert Nellis and Anita Sinner, among others in this collection.

Recently, while editing my students' work, I was surprised to hear John and Carmen's voices offering my students suggestions and encouragement, their voices helping to guide my written words. I wonder if this is the kind of magic that Jean-Paul Restoule mentions in his chapter, or if it is similar to the music that flows through the music people Walter Gershon expresses gratitude for in his chapter, a phenomenon Walter refers to as entanglement. I find as teachers, we can call to our teachers to provide us, and our students, with profound encouragement and guidance. This call, I believe, is heard beyond familiar notions of space and time, perhaps because it is a call powered by love and a special form

Introduction 5

of listening that is made possible by being extraordinarily grateful for lessons received.

I often call to my teachers, I send them an invitation, I accept their gifts, gifts that act as spirits, gifts that I have embraced over the years. I understand that such gifts live in texts and visit and accompany my teaching practice. Many, as Tara-Lynn Scheffel notes in her chapter, reside on bookshelves, or in a book yet to be found. Great teachers inspire teachers, and they journey with us as companions, travelling our landscapes of learning with us, acting as a lasting presence that carries on teaching from teacher to teacher from lifetime to lifetime. This book bears witness to this phenomenon. Such gifts and teachers are referenced through the pages and chapters in this book. Such gifts are living within the text itself, waiting to be channelled into the life of the reader. Like seeds planted in the pages, as a reader, if I can find gratitude for such gifts, I offer fertile ground for growing legacies of learning.

With the current atmosphere brought on by COVID-19, I thought I would find myself writing during a time of contemplation – a time when the world slowed down, but the very opposite came to be true. With the death of George Floyd, a new emotional landscape emerged – a new struggle to find grace. With the significant and revolutionary changes happening in America and around the world – I struggle to find, but still put my faith in, grace. Along with practicing critique, I believe an approach that names gifts, grace and gratitude is an essential method necessary in embracing the ethical core of community, people, relationships, the building blocks of education, while ultimately offering an intimate encounter with the layer of humility that grounds the origin of genius each scholar contributes to this collection. Gifts, grace and gratitude reside in our teaching, in us, and continue to be a presence we pass along. In doing so, in my view, a legacy of learning unfolds.

John

The paragraph above where Adam writes about calling to his teachers offers such a beautiful image/gift. I want to remember/receive that image/gift moving forward with this book as part of my own inspiration for continuing to write, to learn, to teach. For me, I often experience the reverse of what Adam described; without me calling, I hear my teachers calling me. In order to listen, I need spaces that will support my attention. The Sweat Lodge has been one such place. When I was made aware that my maternal grandmother was Aboriginal, I needed to connect with others who would understand the joy and the struggle my body was experiencing. Indigenous friends, colleagues and scholars, among them some of those Adrian Downey writes about in his chapter, helped me find community and begin the process of my own decolonizing; it is a process I am unlikely to finish, but it is a process I will continue.

6 Introduction

Patricia Palulis finds those friends and communities all over the world. Her ability to dwell in each moment and place reflects a deep respect for, and ability to receive the gifts of, the other. Through her images and writing, Fiona Blaikie also brings us up close to the other and to the gifts being offered. There is a feeling of being invited to hold the moment, as much for the other as for oneself.

These days, I remind myself that one I love deeply will, like I did, find her own friends, mentors, communities. Parenting is another way of teaching and learning together. A colleague, after meeting my daughter, told her that I must love her very much because I always generously acknowledge, in my publications, her and my partner's inspiration and support. I do love them both. My choice to name them in my work, however, is one of duty rather than generosity. Being loved and loving opens us to new possibilities and responsibilities. Those possibilities and responsibilities are not imposed; they are, rather, offered and received. I am reminded of Dorothy Vaandering's beautiful acknowledgement of the learning, the gifts, she has received in becoming a parent through adoption, an experience we both share and have often talked about; I am so grateful to see that lived experience now appear so powerfully in Dorothy's writing.

Carmen

In the last several years as I approached retirement, I spent time thinking about what I value most as a curriculum scholar. The word "inquiry" is top of my list because it has been through inquiry that doors have opened for sharing learning that is personal and storied, where heart and soul have mingled in a search for meaning. Embedded in inquiry are questions, attentive listening, responses that draw on lived experience and ultimately, the gift of getting to know something of others' lives from the well of their experience.

Kathryn Ricketts and Avril Aitken have written chapters that point to the gifts that we continue to find as we go forward in our lives as new experiences, including loss, await us. I think back to many events and situations with friends, colleagues, students and others, some who are gone from the world – the list grows with age – who have offered me so many moments of care, love, solace, pleasure and connection, all of which have taught and continue to teach me important lessons about my life and how to be in the world – legacies I hold dear.

Along with inquiry, place is high on my list because curricular encounters are where our experiences are situated. Adam's chapter and my own both focus on places where each of us took steps that shifted the perception we held of the world and ourselves. For me, places hold reference points where I can revisit the past, be thankful for the gifts I received while there, and going forward, remind myself to continue using those

Introduction 7

gifts as I live out the lessons learned with the grace I hope I convey as teacher and learner in the world.

Adam

Anyone who has ever accepted the invitation to teach is gifted an incredible responsibility because inevitably they become part of a legacy of learning. In my view, whether that legacy involves encouragement or discouragement, it is a legacy all the same. Teachers are part of stories that will grow much older and greater than themselves – where their teachings will travel is far beyond the scope of any finite person, or career.

The responsibility of teaching requires grace, I believe. If we can answer the call to be a teacher, we begin a marathon, and we are asked to welcome burdens that we can barely imagine. But through complicated conversations, by searching for the right relationships, the right community, experiences can translate into understandable gifts, and what was once a burden may become a source of gratitude, even moving us closer to who we would like to be. It takes confidence to run towards the gift of being a teacher. I find I am required to embrace who I am, all aspects of who I am honestly, if I am a teacher. This means for me, I need to be confident enough to allow myself and others grace, to receive the gifts offered by embracing who I am.

Carmen, in her chapter, re-visits her younger-self; I enjoyed visiting that Carmen at that age. I visit a younger version of myself in my chapter. I visit him and forgive him; I'm even grateful for what he has offered me, for what he has offered me as a teacher. I believe embracing who we have been with kindness is part of ageing gracefully. It takes strength to do so. In the first chapter of this book, I wonder who John is running towards, as he describes the emotional landscape of his road race, and the distance and diversions, voices and choices that led him towards being the person getting closer to the finish line – or is it a starting line? Teaching involves endurance. What can endure is the stuff of legacy, and I believe what endures is who we truly are. For me, as a teacher and scholar, this means having the courage to describe honestly and openly the hardest lessons we have learned – our teachers are present in such gifts, gifts they leave, gifts they reveal for others. These gifts survive as a legacy, helping others to have the courage, strength or words to unwrap their own legacy of learning.

Nesting this Text in the Broader Field of Curriculum Studies

This text is embedded in a tradition that has blossomed in curriculum studies over the last number of decades where a culture of learning from individuals and their experiences has blossomed. We are fortunate to be able to place this text in a time of openings, where multiple voices are being included in educational research and teaching, where story and

8   *Introduction*

art and poetry continue to emerge as methods and methodologies and where curriculum continues to be translated in new ways by a diversity of scholars in the academy.

Gratitude is the word that comes to mind when thinking about seminal work that informs the pages of this book. Without the individuals and texts noted by authors in each chapter, and the life-long commitment to curriculum development these scholars have provided, our present-day curricular work would not have a strong foundation. It is clear in this text that we reap the benefits of those whose pioneering efforts in curriculum development and research have made our stories of experience, our autobiographies, our histories and uniqueness commonplace in our work. Remembering that these possibilities were not always available is a humble reminder that honouring the personal and academic gifts we have received is a legacy to celebrate and continue in our work.

Carmen

Although I had been a schoolteacher and instructor at the university level for several decades, I confess that my understanding of curriculum was murky at best when I embarked on doctoral study in the early 1990s. Apart from a hazy master's course that highlighted a lot of Ralph Tyler (1969) and very little John Dewey (1938), and school board documents, I arrived at my first doctoral course unable to articulate what I thought curriculum was. Luckily, Michael Connelly was my first instructor and eventually my dissertation supervisor. Gradually, under his mentorship and guidance, my eyes opened to what curriculum could be, and I understood I had a place in my own curriculum development. "Curriculum is a person's life experience," Mick said. I wrote and shared with class colleagues' stories that in Mick's terms were formerly secret or sacred stories, and I began to be brave enough to read my work to my B. Ed. students at my Maritime university.

With this opening, Dewey's notion of attending to "the particular" in life situations, events and experiences took shape for me as I read texts by Carolyn Heilbrun (1988, 1997, 1999), Maxine Greene (1978, 1988, 2000), bell hooks (1989, 1990, 1994, 2000, 2003), Bill Pinar (1994, 1995, 2012, 2015) and others whose work seemed to speak directly to me about my own curricular education. Indeed, serendipity and surprise as expressed by authors in this book were my constant companions as I read widely, absorbed new ways of thinking, wrote copiously and shared with my education students.

Adam

As a pre-service teacher, fresh out of teachers college, I noticed my identity shifting – being shaped, modelled and structured by social forces to meet the high standard any teacher candidate is required to embody as

Introduction 9

they enter the teaching field. During this time, I was wondering what would be left of the unpolished Adam after I finished my teacher training.

The more I thought about the question, the more I realized an uneasy feeling in my gut – that leaving behind or covering up certain aspects of myself to fit the prescription the Ontario College of Teachers expects seemed to me to be symptoms indicating that being a less than perfect person was important, precious and worth holding on to.

As I introspectively explored what becoming part of the educational establishment would mean for me, I read R. D Laing's (1959/1965) *The Divided Self*. In the excitement of becoming a teacher, I couldn't help but notice I was feeling unsettled. As I read Laing's work I associated my teacher training with Laing's descriptions of ontological insecurity, especially with his notions of an un-embodied-self or false-self-system, which Laing believed resulted from an un-dialectical approach to life in which one's inner-self relates to an object rather than people. For me, I recognized the object as school policy. I was proudly entering the teaching field; however, I also felt the consequences of embodying a bureaucratized standard – I felt the consequences of belonging in a school system. Along with becoming a teacher, uncomfortable feelings of futility, meaninglessness, a sense of being unreal resonated within my inner-pre-service-self. I questioned whether the professional standards were ethical, and why I was beginning to feel intellectually empty, wondering why my compliance to the College of Teacher's authority gave me an overall sense of insecurity. Did I belong in the school system?

To academically explore my transformation, I turned to a work by the eminent psychiatrist Carl Jung. Jung's (1957) book titled *The Undiscovered Self* explains a condition which Jung refers to as *organized man* [sic] – a person who lacks a true understanding of her or his inner-self, and relies on statistical truths and abstractions, which push the individual towards committing to a rational and unrealistic representation of the world rather than stepping authentically into the irrational reality that exits outside ideal sentiments and standards. Jung's description hit home; living towards professional standards set by others with disregard for my own inner-wisdom, my own inner-spirit, I felt, would normalize away an important aspect of myself. And I came to believe a neurotic and creatively impotent ethical standard would come to replace my tacit knowledge. I also realized I would have less to offer my students if I was fully committed to presenting myself as ideal – as if I've always lived up to the College's professional standards – I wondered how anyone would be able to relate to someone who did?

I pondered then, what if the College's standards weren't so perfect? I wondered if having such a thought was appropriate for a teacher? I found solace in reading Stanley Milgram's (1974/2009) *Obedience to Authority*, which clearly formulated how a desire to comply to authority could cause regular folk to adopt genocidal behaviours. To further

10   *Introduction*

explore my reservations, before I entered a school as a classroom teacher, I enrolled in a master's degree program that focused on curriculum leadership. Stanley Milgram was a social psychologist, Laing and Jung were psychiatrists and psychoanalysts – they were not schoolteachers.

During the time I was earning my master's degree, I benefited from Dr. Carmen Shields agreeing to be my Supervisor, Carmen introduced me to the field of Narrative Inquiry Self-Study. She became a mentor, colleague and now co-editor. Most importantly, she had a good idea of who I was looking for. That year she introduced me to a collection of essays by William Pinar (1994), titled *Autobiography, politics and sexuality: Essays in curriculum theory 1972–1992*. In the literature, for the first time, I met a teacher and educator, a curriculum theorist – a new mentor-in-text – that had worked through the psychoanalytic literature – addressing existential questions I had as a pre-service teacher, while also offering autobiography as a way to connect authentically with students and myself, by teaching from within.

And finally, and significantly, Pinar introduced me to the work of Ted Tetsuo Aoki (2005). Ted Aoki, for me, is an origin and horizon to be found in Canadian Curriculum Studies. Reading Ted Aoki's (2005) work in *Curriculum in a new key: The collected works of Ted T. Aoki*, a text compiled by William Pinar and Rita Irwin, was a profound curriculum experience that supported my conviction that the lives lived in schools are integral to curriculum development and that identifying and developing a curriculum that is sustainable can only be sustainable if it depends on the biographies lived in a classroom – on a relationship between students and a teacher, as both live the curriculum. Ted Aoki (2005) even had a word for the bureaucratic process I feared I'd succumb to – being *technicized*. His words supported my conviction, to ethically resist the necrophilic urge to dissolve behind the safety of a perfect presentation. What is imperfect is real. In curriculum studies, Pinar and Aoki open a curricular space for what is imperfectly possible, the biographic. Now, scholars in this collection carry on Aoki and Pinar's legacy; Canadian poet-scholars like Carl Leggo (2012) and John Guiney Yallop and Carmen Shields (2017) teach us to live poetically by not worrying whether our poems are perfect, but by paying attention to what they make possible.

John

When a condescending cleric suggested that teaching could be a path for me, after he assumed that by leaving the seminary after one year of theological studies I was leaving the path to priesthood, I decided that I would never become a teacher. Twenty-five years later when I completed my Master of Education degree, and after almost two decades working as an elementary school educator, my partner, more lovingly and with

Introduction 11

more knowledge of whom he was speaking to, told me that he wanted me to go on with my studies. I decided that I would become an academic.

During my M.Ed., Susan Drake (1992) introduced me to Narrative Inquiry in a course at Brock University, and I walked through a new door of possibility. Carmen Shields (1997) was on the other side of that door; she invited me to go further into what was possible. Carmen introduced me to the works of Jean Clandinin and Michael Connelly (1991, 1994, 1995, 2000). I learned how to think and write narratively. I learned that my stories mattered. I learned that those stories were more than repeated memories of lived experience, that they could also be educative for me and for others.

While how to do my research was what I was looking for as I began my graduate studies, what I wanted to research was clear to me before I started. I wanted to understand why schools were such homophobic environments, and what I could do to help transform schools into more welcoming spaces for sexual minority and gender diverse students, parents and teachers. Consequently, gay, lesbian and queer-identified authors (Chase, 1998; D'Augelli, 1994, 1996, 1998; Dorais, 1992 Lipkin, 1995, 1999; Savin-Williams, 1995, 1998; Sears, 1997) became important educators and supporters for me as I worked to do what may have been the impossible. With stories generously shared by two participants, an out gay student and a closeted gay teacher, I, an out gay activist elementary school teacher, inquired into their and my narratives of fear, relief, sadness, joy, loss, empowerment and becoming.

I do not know the impact of my M.Ed. research (Guiney, 2002), if any, on others, but I do know its impact on me. It changed me. It made me understand that I could not be a voice for others, but I could help others find their own voices. It made me understand that the only person I can change is myself, and I could then offer to others what I previously could not...most likely because previously I was unaware, ignorant, of what was possible, of what I could do. I came to understand that my stories could be told and retold, and that each telling and retelling could open doors of possibility, just as a door of possibility had been opened for me.

When I began my doctoral studies, I was less ambitious. I was, perhaps, more humble. Autoethnographers (Bochner & Ellis, 1996; Ellis, 1997; Ellis & Bochner, 2000; Rambo Ronai, 1996; Tillman-Healy, 1996), poetic inquirers (Cahnmann, 2003; Davis Halifax et al., 2004; Leggo, 1994, 2001, 2004, 2005, 2007) and, again, queer theorists (Foucault, 1990; Kumashiro, 2002; McNinch & Cronin, 2004; Sedwick, 1990; Tierney, 1997) helped me better understand what was possible. They helped me better understand myself and my identities, and the communities in which or outside of which I live those identities. They also helped me realize how that understanding of self, offered through the emotional language of poetry, could open up new doors of possibility for others.

12 *Introduction*

What those, and more, authors throughout my graduate studies gave me was not only a foundation to build on, but also a home to live in. They made it possible for me to see the world as a place for me to live and work, a place that I could reclaim, and a place where I could belong. I remain deeply grateful.

Carmen

Today, as I sit by my bookshelves I see many authors whose work has been seminal for me over my many years as an academic. Some I have met, while others remain in Heilbrun's (1997) words, "unmet friends." I see the life's work of Connelly, (1988); Clandinin & Connelly, (1991, 1994, 1995, 2000); Clandinin, (2007, 2013), William Pinar (1994, 1995, 2009, 2011, 2012, 2015), William Doll Jr. (1993), and Parker Palmer (1998, 1993, 2000, 2004, 2018), all of whom have challenged and changed my thinking and subsequent choices as a teacher and researcher. I see the work of Denzin and Lincoln (2000, 2005, 2018) and I remember participating in the conferences Norman Denzin held at his university that opened doors for international curriculum scholars to share their own research experience in a multitude of ways including story, poetry and dance. I see the qualitative research texts I have used with my graduate students – Cynthia Chambers et al. (2012), Corrine Glesne (2011) and more recently, Sharon Merriam and Elizabeth Tisdell's (2016) books among them – and I realize that I am part of the legacy of all these scholars now, as I hope in some small way, I am in the lives of those who have studied with me.

Over many years my graduate students have kept me reading widely and writing my research contributions consistently for our Canadian Association for Curriculum Studies conferences and beyond, in my attempt to continue my own learning and also support and guide their interests, their research topics and the methodologies that fit their work. My students have presented me with topics such as coming out, head injury, reviving the spirit, soul work, bereavement, heritage, adoption, immigration tales and personal philosophy – each student I have supervised has helped me see my world in new ways and I am grateful to each one.

I have added numerous research texts to my bookshelf to accompany those I mentioned above. For example, scholarly work by John Guiney Yallop (2017, 2020), and Carl Leggo (1999, 2012); Pauline Sameshima (2007); Ardra Cole and Gary Knowles (2008); Shaun McNiff (1998, 2011) and Rita Irwin (2013) among many others rest on my shelves; all have helped me reflect the vision, history, culture and experience of the graduate students I have been blessed to work with.

In the present there are now many authors I could mention who inhabit the educational research and curriculum worlds noted here – like me, former students of these ground-breaking individuals or curricular friends made because of common subjects and interests. They

Introduction 13

write, draw, paint and perform their work making the whole field of education richer, more poignant, more personal and connected to the lives we live.

John

After reading my previous section immediately above, Carmen replied via email telling me that I would have to write for this introduction again (one last time), that I would need to move up to the present and write about the academic I am today. The academic I am today? Dare I? I think not. I think I will leave that for a future work, one that I am addressing alongside this project as I come to recognize the less generous aspects of the academic world and their effects on me despite my efforts to respond to or resist them in constructive, positive ways. What I can write about is the community that welcomed me, that embraced me, that supported me, that not only opened and held a space for my voice but also allowed me to hold spaces for their voices.

I wrote elsewhere (Hasebe-Ludt & Leggo, 2018) about my inadvertent entry into the Canadian Association for Curriculum Studies. What I did not write about is the community, the Special Interest Group, within that organization that really caught my attention. The Arts Researchers and Teachers Society (ARTS, such a lovely acronym), not only welcomed my scholarship, they also sought my leadership. I served on the Executive for six years (two each as Vice-President, President and Past-Present). In those first years, I came to know scholars, both those with much experience and those who were novices, whose work, passion and kindness moved and inspired me. Among those who welcomed my work alongside theirs were Monica Prendergast, Carl Leggo and Pauline Sameshima (2009), Diane Conrad and Anita Sinner (2015), Kathleen Galvin (Galvin & Prendergast, 2016). Nicholas Ng-a-Fook (Ng-a-Fook, Ibrahim, & Reis, 2016) was a frequent welcoming presence in the Curriculum Studies community I had entered. As well as the respect I felt from him for my work, his warm smile and strong hugs always reminded me that I belonged. These scholars were carving out space in the academic world for individuals who used the arts in research. Some of them very specifically had carved out a space for my art – poetry. Monica Prendergast, with Carl Leggo, held an International Symposium on Poetic Inquiry (later known as ISPI), to which I was invited. When I presented my work at the symposium, Monica very passionately and beautiful described my work alongside Carl Leggo's as paying homage to the sacrifice parents make for their children. I was home. Since that time, I have attended every biennial ISPI and co-hosted two of them. It is the only multi-day academic event I have attended where the entire program is consecutive, allowing all participants to participate in every session. Every person, yes every person, who has attended and presented

14 *Introduction*

at an ISPI has had a significant impact on my work as an academic. I am grateful for each one of them.

Adam

The first line in the forward in Patricia Liu Baergen's work *Tracing Ted Tetsuo Aoki's Intellectual Formation* begins with Pinar stating Ted Tetsuo Aoki is a Legend. Of equal importance, Pinar balances this statement by describing Ted Aoki as a husband to June, father of Edward and Douglas, along with other particulars of his personhood. Patricia Liu Baergen (2020) speaks of generations of curriculum scholars, administrators and teachers influenced by Ted Aoki (Also see, Hurren & Hasebe-Ludt, 2014).

As I mentioned earlier, to me, Ted Aoki is a horizon, beyond Western Canada his intellectual efforts illuminate the epistemological topography of the Canadian Curriculum landscape (Baergen, 2020). The poetic ponderings of Aoki's mentee, Carl Leggo, reflect the influence of Aokian linguistics (Leggo, 2018). Carl's ponderings are vitalizing new landscapes; scholars like Carl Leggo (2012), and those inspired by him, I believe – along with Patricia Liu Baergen (2020), continue to answer Cynthia Chambers (1999) call for a unique theoretical language in Canadian curriculum theory – a language I hear taking sound.

Perhaps because of the high quality of Aoki's work and scholars like Baergen (2020), and Chambers (1999), I feel less like an alienated outsider out of place – I want to acknowledge that I feel a strong sense of what is involved in being a Canadian curriculum scholar. A trembling ontology, (Ng-A-Fook, 2014), for me, is a reverberation resulting from attuning to openings, to what is between, from provoking such spaces (Strong-Wilson, 2020). In my experience, a continuous contextual shift is normative, at times, even often, unsettling and painful. Listening, interdependence, generative tension(s), gratitude and grace, and a sense of humour, while striving for a certain sense of independence, community, openness, even fun, keeps my Canadian identity in place. I try to be polite, too.

I work to recognize Canada's history of colonization and my own privilege as an individual with settler heritage. I acknowledge my need to work, listen, learn and engage in a process of decolonization. People in the community where I teach have helped me with this, people like Ruth Quesnelle and Jeff Monague – for me, this process involves people and community and can't rely only on scholarly texts.

Since Hodgetts's (1968) study on Canadian culture and heritage in education, much work has been done in the search of Canadian ways of knowing. The work continues. Recently, a colleague and I read through the Indigenous Peoples Atlas of Canada (2018), her historical community, the Métis having migrated from Drummond Island

Introduction 15

to Penetanguishene, is largely absent from the Atlas's topography and narrative. Our stories are important, when including I believe it is crucial to be careful not to suggest a space is definitive. In holding a space – in assuming it's authoritative, I feel ignorance is risked if a relationship isn't continued with what is outside familiar boundaries – perhaps the heart of a curriculum is kept healthy by a relationship between boundaries. There is the arrogance of gift, especially in terms of belonging, "its certainties, presumptions, and commitments," a concept articulated by Madeleine Grumet in the forward to *Provoking Curriculum Encounters Across Educational Experience* (Strong-Wilson, 2020). For me, the arrogance of gift, attempting to be aware of it, is an essential responsibility I commit to in terms of how I study Canadian Curriculum theory.

What is of worth, in the Origin of Canadian scholarship, I believe, is a presence practiced in the present. Through study, a presence of scholars past, is left with us, in us. As a Canadian scholar, I see theoretical language that is uniquely Canadian, a language that is not exclusively intentionally unique but unique by the very fact that it can't help but be; heritage, race, gender distinctiveness is brought to being; unique in curriculum found in family history, ethnicity, nationality, gender identity; medicine found in our diversity – in the pain found there too, found in the past in our present, in our struggles, in our imperfections and invitations and imaginations, in our writing, in our gifts and grace. A language is offered in the pages that follow. I try to avoid saying "we as Canadians." In our multi-personhood, our multi-nationality, you will find some traditionally Canadian colloquiums in this text, like the Canadian standoff between Fiona Blaikie and Ted Aoki, but I believe theoretical strength is in an attempt to engage in conversation that requires instances where we recognize we are rarely the same – in doing so we potentially uncover lessons, gifts of learning found contextually, uniquely, in one another's experiences. In this text, scholars share personal views, struggles, influences, understandings of curriculum encounters – they share their experience of being curriculum theorists.

Beckoning for serendipity, for magic, eager as learners, eager as listeners, eager for possibilities in the pages that follow – are elements of a language I hear calling to me as I read through this text. Pinar asks us to work from within. If I dig deep to my very core I find a spiral staircase, spinning relentlessly, being reconstructed and carrying on body to body to some future time. As teachers, we have lessons, we express them to our students, and we hope they go on to benefit from our teachings.

What is divine about teaching and scholarship, perhaps, can be cited in sources, but I believe it is more accurately described as being found in people, in communities, – Carmen and her presence in my life, John who is largely responsible for my perspective on poetry – their teacherness,

16 Introduction

I have inherited to a degree. How much of a teaching legacy belongs to the genius of an individual? With a discerning gaze, I imagine very little. Of course, a teacher falls shy of the western myth of the heroic individual. But within our individualism is one of our greatest gifts, the unique experiential existence that is exclusive to our biography – the life learning only we can contribute and claim; its beauty, its haunting fragility, originality, the totality of its remarkableness, belongs to our individual lives.

As a student of science, I'm in awe at the discovery of the genome, as a poet, I view the spiral staircase as a metaphor for legacies of learning. Each teacher providing rungs of the spiral steps.

From Jung (1957) I learned to value and respect my own process of *individuation*. I see and I feel a tension between the individual and social elements of one's, my, Self-as-learner. From Aoki (2005), I came to appreciate the vitalizing tensions, *generative tensions,* I see, I feel, as I evolve through that process – as I exist not merely as an individual, but also contextually and culturally as a social being living in my community. I believe a scholar like Ted Aoki is an inspiration and that he influences curriculum theorists because he asks us to question what is static – the "timeless truths" – to be aware of where and who we are – in *relation*. Born of one another through conversation, if done respectfully, we experience intercourse – the most primal and primaeval form of education, natural and beautiful, through which legacies of learning spiral and climb towards the greatest mysteries, towards human aspirations and achievements, towards human potential itself.

If we refuse to be standardized in our approach to curriculum by embracing complexity, acknowledging inequity and humbling ourselves to avoid destroying our individual and cultural uniqueness and the accomplishments of our teachers before us, lessons from our lives can shine. To wake up to our potential, to learn to listen to what our own writing needs – do we need teachers? Teachers like the ones mentioned in this text, like teachers you the reader may already have encountered?

If you chose to be a teacher – lessons are abundant in this book, in relationships, in the genius of our species belonging to the legacy of learning passed along by teachers past and present, not belonging to the work of any one teacher, but to the presence of lives lived learning through the ages. A teacher is not merely a body, but a presence that exists and is appreciated long after the body is gone.

The core of great teaching belongs to the work of teachers collectively through human history, we summon their efforts into our practice. Legacy is not what has been left behind, but belongs to an audience, feeling, listening and investing in the emotional journey to inspire to carry on what is in our power to teach to change the world.

Introduction 17

References

Aoki, T. (2005). Teaching as in-dwelling between two curriculum worlds. In W. Pinar & R. Irwin (Eds.), *Curriculum in a new key: The collected works of Ted T. Aoki* (pp. 159–165). Mahwah, NJ: Lawrence Erlbaum.

Baergen, P. (2020). *Tracing Ted Tetsuo Aoki's intellectual formation (Studies in Curriculum Theory Series)*. New York, NY: Taylor and Francis. Kindle Edition.Bochner, A. P., & Ellis, C. (1996). Talking over autoethnography. In C. Ellis & A. P. Bochner (Eds.), *Composing ethnography: Alternative forms of qualitative research* (pp. 13–45). Walnut Creek, CA: AltaMira.

Cahnmann, M. (2003). The craft, practice, and possibility of poetry in educational research. *Educational Researcher*, Volume 32, Issue 3, (April), 29–36.

Canadian Geographic Indigenous Peoples Atlas of Canada (2018). The Royal Canadian Geographical Society.

Chambers, C. M., Hasebe-Ludt, E., Leggo, C., & Sinner, A. (Eds.), (2012). *A heart of wisdom: Life writing as empathetic inquiry*. New York, NY: Peter Lang.

Chambers, C. (1999). A topography for Canadian curriculum theory. *Canadian Journal of Education*, 24(2), 137–150.

Chase, C. (1998). Introduction. In C. Chase (Ed.), *Queer 13: Lesbian and gay writers recall seventh grade* (pp. xii–xv). New York, NY: Rob Weisbach Books.

Clandinin, D. J. (2013). *Engaging in narrative inquiry*. Walnut creek, CA: Left Coast Press.

Clandinin, D. J. (2007). *Handbook of narrative inquiry*. Thousand Oaks, CA: Sage.

Clandinin, D. J., & Connelly, F. M. (2000). *Narrative inquiry: Experience and story in qualitative research*. San Francisco, CA: Jossey-Bass.

Clandinin, D. J., & Connelly, F. M. (1995). *Teachers' professional knowledge landscapes*. New York, NY: Teachers College Press.

Clandinin, D. J., & Connelly, F. M. (1994). Personal experience methods. In N. K. Denzin & Y. S. Lincoln (Eds.), *Handbook of Qualitative Research* (pp. 413–444). Thousand Oaks, CA: Sage.

Clandinin, D. J., & Connelly, F. M. (1991). Narrative and story in practice and research. In D. Schon (Ed.), *The reflective turn: Case studies in and on educational research* (pp. 258–281). New York, NY: Teachers College Press.

Cole, A. L., & Knowles, J. G. (2008). *Handbook of the arts in qualitative research*. Thousand Oaks, CA: Sage.

Connelly, F. M., & Clandinin, D. J. (1988). *Teachers as curriculum planners: Narratives of experience*. New York, NY: Teachers College Press.

Conrad, D. and Sinner, A. (Eds.). (2005). *Creating together: Participatory, community-based, and collaborative arts practices and scholarship across Canada*. Waterloo: Wilfred Laurier University Press.

D'Augelli, A. R. (1998). Developmental implications of victimization of lesbian, gay, and bisexual youth. In G. M. Herek (Ed.), *Stigma and sexual orientation: Understanding prejudice against lesbians, gay men, and bisexuals* (pp. 187–210). Thousand Oaks, CA: Sage.

D'Augelli, A. R. (1996). Lesbian, gay, and bisexual development during adolescence and young adulthood. In R. P. Cabaj & T. S. Stein (Eds.), *Textbook of homosexuality and mental health* (pp. 267–288). Washington, DC: American Psychiatric Press.

18   *Introduction*

D'Augelli, A. R. (1994). Lesbian and gay male development: Steps toward an analysis of lesbians' and gay men's lives. In B. Greene & G. M. Herek (Eds.), *Lesbian and gay psychology: Theory, research and clinical applications* (pp. 118–132). Thousand Oaks, CA: Sage.

Davis Halifax, N., Brown, B., Compton, V., & O'Connor, M. A. (2004). Imagination, walking – In/Forming Theory. In A. L. Cole, L. Neilsen, J. G. Knowles & T T. C. Luciani (Eds.), *Provoked by art: Theorizing arts-informed research* (pp. 175–187). Halifax, NS: Backalong Books.

Denzin, N. K., & Lincoln, Y. S. (Eds.), (2000). *Handbook of qualitative research.* Thousand Oaks, CA: Sage.

Denzin, N. K., & Lincoln, Y. S. (Eds.), (2005). *Sage handbook of qualitative research* (3rd ed.), Thousand Oaks, CA: Sage.

Denzin, N. K., & Lincoln, Y. S. (Eds.), (2018). *Sage handbook of qualitative research* (5th ed.), Thousand Oaks, CA: Sage.

Dewey, J. (1938). *Experience and education.* New York, NY: Collier.

Doll, W. E. Jr. (1993). *A post-modern perspective on curriculum.* New York, NY: Teachers College press.

Dorais, M. (1992). *Mort our fif: Contextes et mobiles de tentatives de suicide chez des adolescents et jeunes hommes homosexuels our identifiés comme tells.* Québec: Centre de Recherches sur les Services Communautaires, Université Laval.

Drake, S. M. (1992). Personal transformation: A guide for the female hero. *Women & Therapy, 12*(3), 51–65.

Ellis, C., & Bochner, A. P. (2000). Autoethnography, Personal Narrative, Reflexivity: Researcher as Subject. In N. K. Denzin & Y. S. Lincoln (Eds.), *Handbook of Qualitative Research* (pp. 733–786). Thousand Oaks, CA: Sage.

Ellis, C. (1997). Evocative autoethnography: Writing emotionally about our lives. In W. G. Tierney & Y. S. Lincoln (Eds.), *Representation and the text: Re-framing the narrative voice* (pp. 115–139). Albany: State University of New York Press.

Foucault, M. (1990). *The history of sexuality: An introduction, Volume 1.* New York, NY: Vintage Books.

Galvin, K., & Prendergast, M. (Eds.). (2016). *Poetic Inquiry II: Seeing, Understanding, Caring: Using Poetry as and for Inquiry.* Netherlands: Sense Publishers.

Glesne, C. (2011). *Becoming qualitative researchers* (4th ed.), Boston, MA: Allyn & Bacon.

Greene, M. (2000). *Releasing the imagination: Essays on education, the arts, and social change.* San Francisco, CA: Jossey-Bass.

Greene, M. (1988). *The dialectic of freedom.* New York, NY: Teachers College Press.

Greene, M. (1978). *Landscapes of learning.* New York, NY: Teachers College Press.

Guiney, J. J. (2002). *School life for gays: A critical study through story.* Unpublished M.Ed. Research Project, St. Catharines, Ontario: Brock University.

Guiney Yallop, J. J. (2020). *Travelling with my daughter.* Monee, IL: An Amazon Publication

Guiney Yallop, J. J., & Shields, C. (2017). The art of teaching rests in connection. In S. Wiebe, E. Lyle, P. Wright, K. Dark, M. McLarnon & L. Day (Eds.), *Ways of being in teaching: Conversations and reflections.* (pp. 87–100). Sense Publications.

Introduction 19

Hasebe-Ludt, E., & Leggo, C. (2018). *Canadian Curriculum Studies: A Métissage of inspiration/imagination/interconnection.* Toronto: Canadian Scholars.

Heilbrun, C. (1999). *Women's lives: The view from the threshold.* Toronto, ON: University of Toronto Press.

Heilbrun, C. (1997). *The last gift of time: Life beyond sixty.* New York, NY: Ballantine.

Heilbrun, C. (1988). *Writing a woman's life.* New York, NY: W.W. Norton & Company.

Hodgetts, A. B. (1968). *What culture? What heritage? A study of civic education in Canada.* Toronto: Ontario Institute for Studies in Education.

hooks, b. (2003). *Teaching community: A pedagogy of hope.* New York, NY: Routledge.

hooks, b. (2000). *Where we stand: Class matters.* New York, NY: Routledge.

hooks, b. (1994). *Teaching to transgress: Education as the practice of freedom.* New York, NY: Routledge.

hooks, b. (1990). *Yearnings: Race, gender, and cultural politics.* Toronto, ON: Between the Lines.

hooks, b. (1989). *Talking back.* Toronto, ON: Between the Lines.

Hurren, W., & Hasebe-Ludt, E. (2014). Preface: An invitation to contemplate the topos and humus of curriculum and genealogical grounds: A Festschrift/Gedenkschrift for Ted Tetsuo Aoki. In W. Hurren & E. Hasebe-Ludt Edition. (Eds.), *Contemplating curriculum: Genealogies/times/places* (pp. xiii–xvii). New York, NY: Routledge.

Irwin, Rita L. (2013) Becoming A/r/tography. *Studies in Art Education, 54*(3), 198–215, DOI: 10.1080/00393541.2013.11518894

Jung, C. (1957). *The undiscovered self* (R. C. Hull, Trans.). New York, NY: Mentor Books.

Kumashiro, K. (2002). *Troubling education: Queer activism and antioppressive pedagogy.* New York, NY: Routledge.

Laing, R. D. (1965). *The divided self.* London, UK: Pelican Books. (Original work published 1959).

Leggo, C. (2018). Loving language: Poetry, curriculum, and Ted T. Aoki. *Alberta Journal of Educational Research, 64*(1), 14–34.

Leggo, C. (2012). Living Language. What is a poem good for? *Journal of the Canadian Association for Curriculum Studies, 10*(1), 141–160.

Leggo, C. (2007). *Come-by-chance: A collection of poems.* St. John's, NL: Breakwater.

Leggo, C. (2005). Pedagogy of the heart: Ruminations on living poetically. *Journal of Educational Thought, 39*(2), 175–195.

Leggo, C. (2004). Living poetry: Five ruminations. *Language & literacy: A Canadian Educational E-Journal [Online], 6*(2), [unpaginated]. Available at http://www.langandlit.ualberta.ca.

Leggo, C. (2001). Research as poetic rumination: Twenty-six ways of listening to light. In L. Neilsen, A. L. Cole & J. G. Knowles (Eds.), *The art of writing inquiry* (pp. 173–195). Halifax, NS: Backalong Books.

Leggo, C. (1994). *Growing up perpendicular on the side of a hill.* St. John's, NL: Killick Press.

Lipkin, A. (1999). *Understanding homosexuality, changing schools: A text for teachers, counselors, and administrators.* Boulder, CO: Westview Press.

20 *Introduction*

Lipkin, A. (1995). The case of a gay and lesbian curriculum. In G. Unks (Ed.), *The gay teen: Educational practice and theory for lesbian, gay, and bisexual adolescents* (pp. 31–52). New York, NY: Routledge.

McNinch, J., & Cronin, M. (Eds.) (2004). *I could not speak my heart: Education and social justice for gay and lesbian youth.* Regina, SK: Canadian Plains Research Center.

McNiff, S. (1998). *Art-based research.* London, UK: Jessica Kingsley Publishers.

McNiff, S. (2011). Artistic expressions as primary modes of inquiry. *British Journal of Guidance & Counselling, 39*(5), 385–396.

Merriam, S., & Tisdell, E.J. (2016). *Qualitative research* (4th ed), San Francisco, CA: Jossey-Bass.

Milgram, S. (2009). *Obedience to authority.* New York, NY: Harper & Row. (Original work published 1974).

Ng-A-Fook, N. (2014). Provoking the very "idea" of Canadian curriculum studies as a counterpointed composition. *Journal of the Canadian Association for Curriculum Studies, 12*(1), 10– 69.

Ng-a-Fook, N., Ibrahim, A., & Reis, G. (Eds.). (2016). *Provoking curriculum studies: Strong poetry and the arts of the possible in education.* New York, NY: Routledge.

Palmer, P. (2018). *On the brink of everything.* Oakland, CA: Berrett-Koehler Publishers.

Palmer, P. (2004). *A hidden wholeness.* San Francisco, CA: Jossey-Bass.

Palmer, P. (2000). *Let your life speak.* San Francisco, CA: Jossey-Bass.

Palmer, P. (1998). *The courage to teach: Exploring the inner landscape of a teacher's life.* San Francisco, CA: Jossey-Bass.

Palmer, P. (1993). *To know as we are known: Education as a spiritual journey.* New York, NY: HarperCollins.

Pinar, W. F. (2011). *The character of curriculum studies: Bildung, currere, and the recurring question of the subject.* New York, NY: Palgrave Macmillan.

Pinar, W. F. (2015). *Educational experience as lived: Knowledge, history, alterity.* New York, NY: Routledge.

Pinar, W. F., & Grumet, M. (2015). *Toward a poor curriculum.* Kingston, NY: Educator's International Press.

Pinar, W. F. (2012). *What is curriculum theory?* New York, NY: Routledge.

Pinar, W. F., Reynolds, W. M., Slattery, P., & Taubman, P. M. (1995). *Understanding curriculum.* New York, NY: Peter Lang.

Pinar, W. F. (1994). *Autobiography, politics and sexuality: Essays in curriculum theory 1972–1992.* New York, NY: Peter Lang.

Prendergast, M, Leggo, C., & Sameshima, P. (Eds.). (2009). *Poetic Inquiry: Vibrant voices in the social sciences.* Rotterdam, The Netherlands: SensePublishers.

Rambo Ronai, C. (1996). My mother is mentally retarded. In C. Ellis & A. P. Bochner (Eds.), *Composing ethnography: Alternative forms of qualitative writing* (pp. 109–131). Walnut Creek, CA: AltaMira.

Sameshima, P. (2007). *Seeing red.* Amherst, NY: Cambria Press.

Savin-Williams, R. C. (1998). *And then I became gay: Young men's stories.* New York, NY: Routledge.

Savin-Williams, R. C. (1995). Lesbian, gay male and bisexual adolescents: In A. R. D'Augelli & C. J. Patterson (Eds.), *Lesbian, gay, and bisexual identities over the life span: Psychological perspectives* (pp. 165–189). New York, NY: Oxford University Press.

Introduction 21

Sears, J. T. (1997). Thinking critically/interviewing effectively about heterosexism and homophobia. A twenty-five year research retrospective. In J. T. Sears & w. L. Williams (Eds.), *Overcoming heterosexism and homophobia: Strategies that work* (pp. 14–48). New York, NY: Columbia University Press.

Sedwick, E. K. (1990). *Epistemology of the closet*. Berkeley and Los Angeles, CA: University of California Press.

Shields, C. (1997). *Behind objective description: Special education and the reality of lived experiences. Unpublished doctoral* thesis, University of Toronto.

Strong-Wilson, T., Ehret, C., Lewkowich, D., & Chang-Kredl, S. (2020). *Provoking curriculum encounters across educational experience (Studies in Curriculum Theory Series)*. Taylor and Francis. Kindle Edition.

Tierney, W. G. (1997). *Academic outlaws: Queer theory and cultural studies in the academy*. Thousand Oaks, CA: Sage.

Tillman-Healy, L. M. (1996). A secret life in a culture of thinness: Reflections on body, food, and bulimia. In C. Ellis & A. P. Bochner (Eds.), *Composing ethnography: Alternative forms of qualitative writing* (pp. 76–108). Walnut Creek, CA: AltaMira.

Tyler, R. (1969). *Basic principles of curriculum and instruction*. Chicago, IL: University of Chicago Press.

1 I am Grateful for Every Invitation

John J. Guiney Yallop

Several years ago, my niece Wendy invited me to run a 10-mile (16-kilometre) road race with her and some other family members and friends. I had not run in many years because running caused me to have severe pains in my knees. I decided, however, with new well-designed running shoes, to try it. I gave myself six months to prepare. The first kilometre of training was hard, the second not easier, and after the third I wanted to give up, but even more I wanted to follow through on my acceptance of the invitation from/for Wendy, and for myself. I finished the road race, and that was my goal – to finish. What I did not expect was that I would begin to like running again; I rediscovered how moving made me feel. I thought, "What further running goals can I work towards?" I decided to run a marathon before my sixtieth birthday. In 2018, more than three years after I began running again, and less than a year from my sixtieth birthday, I ran a marathon.

As I look back on my life, in particular on my life in the education and academic communities, so much of my growth and learning, especially my learning about myself, has been in response to invitations. Much of what I wrote about in the introduction with Carmen and Adam was invitations. The invitation to Narrative Inquiry extended by Susan Drake, which was taken up by Carmen Shields, an invitation she continued, in many forms, throughout my M.Ed. program and research. The invitation by Monica Prendergast to the International Symposium on Poetic Inquiry (ISPI). Prior to that, in a Directed Study course with my PhD dissertation supervisor, Cornelia Hoogland invited me to write only poetry for my assignments. Joy, like love, comes with responsibility. I do not think I worked so hard on anything prior to that, and I had never written so much poetry in one block of time before as I did in that course and in my subsequent work on my dissertation. In the past, my writing had come in spurts, in moments of crisis, when I needed to write. For my doctoral research, writing was a duty. I embraced that duty like the good Catholic I once was and with an intention of perseverance and a prayer for discernment. The Poetic Inquiry community, found mostly among the many poet scholars who attended the seven ISPIs over the years of

DOI: 10.4324/9781003154112-2

I am Grateful for Every Invitation   23

this biennial gathering, not only invited me to join them in community, in writing, they also made my work part of their work.

One member of that poetic scholarly community, Carl Leggo, was particularly welcoming and generous. Carl, at times a colleague, a friend, a confidant, a wise counsellor, invited me to practice generosity...always. And it was/is a practice, something I keep practicing, keep getting better at and keep slipping away from, a practice to which I keep returning. Generosity is a space where I can best remember Carl. When he was dying, we emailed a few times. We joked about the shared experience of having a MRI. "I eagerly agree that a MRI is one of the strangest experiences I have had!" he wrote on January 31st in 2019. He died just over a month later, on March 7. We once wrote a poem together. Back and forth over email we sent a verse each time until one of us said it was done. Done. When we are done with life, or life is done with us, what is left? Carl left a legacy of love and generosity. Readers of this publication will have seen his name in the introduction and they will see it frequently in chapters following this one.

I need to return to the marathon I ran less than a year before Carl died. Unlike the ISPI that I attended in 2007, my marathon will not be my first marathon; it will be my marathon, my only marathon. I do not need another marathon, no more than I need to write another dissertation or prepare another application for tenure or promotion to associate or full professor. In some ways, however, running my marathon revealed to me more unexpected things about myself than my dissertation or any of my applications for tenure or promotion have. Perhaps, because my body was so fully engaged in running my marathon, it took me into parts of my emotional landscape I could not go into with my mind and heart no matter how much I thought I was also engaging my body in my writing. Writing a doctoral dissertation and writing applications for tenure and promotion taught me about gratitude for what I have accomplished, the gifts I have received and for those who have supported me in my journeys. Running my marathon, however, taught me about another path to gratitude, a kind of gratitude I did not know I could, or even wanted to, experience and a path I did not know I needed to travel.

Once I began my marathon, like with my dissertation and my applications for tenure and promotion, I knew that I would finish it unless I was, through serious injury or death, taken out of the race. That is not to suggest that my marathon or my dissertation or my applications for promotion were without pain. I experienced much pain in each, but, in the marathon, and perhaps the dissertation, it was pain that needed to be acknowledged, pain that I needed to feel, pain I had to push through in order to come to the understandings I would arrive at both in and through each experience. During my marathon, I got lost for a short while. I followed pylons up steps to a space that had no exit. I called a friend who had run many marathons. He told me to look around until

24   *John J. Guiney Yallop*

I could see other runners. I did, and I ran down the steps I had run up and followed two other runners. I sometimes joke that I actually ran more than a marathon because of that "detour." Similarly, with my applications for tenure and promotion I also felt lost at times. I called experienced friends who guided me back to where I needed to be. In some ways, my applications were also probably more than they needed to be. That is not an unusual experience for marginalized academics; we overcompensate for what we perceive to be our inadequacies, our defects, our unworthiness.

I passed the 39th kilometre marker. Just 3.2 kilometres and I will have finished a marathon. I saw the 40th kilometre marker up ahead. Suddenly, I felt a ball inside me; it felt like it was in my stomach, in my gut. It was not a baseball or a soccer ball; it felt more like one of those large exercise balls that became, for a while, popular as seats to improve posture and decrease back pain. It hurt. I heard voices from the ball. They were not the voices of encouragement or support to which I had become accustomed and for which I was grateful. They were the voices of people who had told me that I would never amount to anything because I was "just a faggot." They were the voices of people who told me that I would never have any real friends, never find someone to love me, never have a job like "normal people," and never have children. I would never accomplish anything or have anything or anyone of value in my life because I was just a faggot, I was just a queer, and I was not worthy of anything except the crap that would inevitably come my way. It was raining; the drops of rain mixed with the tears on my face as I cried while I ran.

How could those voices still be in me...now? I thought I had, many years before, gotten rid of those voices with those hateful and hurtful messages; I thought I had left them behind. Why was I hearing them, again, and why now? I received emails from family and friends before the marathon began, wishing me well. I received text messages during the marathon, again encouraging me. The friend I called when I was lost gently and lovingly guided me back on track. I was married to someone I loved deeply and who deeply loved me. We parented our beautiful daughter who adored both of us. I had had two successful careers, and I had just recently received a letter informing me of my promotion to the highest rank in the second one. And today, today I will finish a marathon!

"Fuck them!"

Those two words were my first thought about, and in response to, the voices I was hearing. Those two words, however, were more an angry reaction and frustrated attempt to get rid of, or away from, those voices again, than they were an expression of what I was feeling more deeply. What was I feeling more deeply, besides this ball in my gut? I continued to run. I had passed the 40th marker and I could see the 41st marker up ahead.

I am Grateful for Every Invitation 25

It was forgiveness. I was feeling forgiveness. I was feeling forgiveness for the people who had spoken those words to or about me, and I was feeling forgiveness for myself for holding onto those voices, for allowing them to stay inside me for so long. As I passed the 41st marker, the huge ball moved up through my body and out through the top of my head. As I continued to run, I heard nothing except my breath, and the voice of the police officer telling me that I was almost there, and I felt nothing except the mist on my face from the light rain. Well, I felt something else. I felt grateful as I ran towards the finish line, where my daughter was waiting, after finishing her 10-kilometre race, to run the last metres of my marathon with me.

I have thought many times since that day about that experience during the last few kilometres of my marathon; on very few occasions, I have shared it with others. It was not until editing this collection, however, and reading comments on my work, both present and previous, from my two co-editors, that I realized that forgiveness is grace, that grace (forgiveness) is a path to gratitude. I realized that if I am to fully use the gifts in my life, with gratitude for them, then I need to continue to practice grace, to show grace, even in times and places and to people, or perhaps especially, when, where and to whom I do not feel particularly inclined to show grace. Perhaps, now, more than ever, as I look to the final years of my second career, in a time when our communities struggle with, and with how to respond to, violence and fear in their many manifestations, I need to show grace. More precisely perhaps, at a time of such brokenness, the world needs more grace and I have a responsibility to give it.

I am grateful to Wendy for the invitation to run a road race with her, and with other family members and friends. I am grateful for every invitation before and after. I am particularly grateful for the invitation I heard that day of my marathon, through the voices that had caused so much pain, and very likely, because of the other voices throughout my life that have shown so much love. I heard a call to respond to violence with forgiveness, with grace, and to continue to live my life with gratitude for the many gifts I have received. Perhaps what I am realizing, finally, is that what I have been doing, or attempting to do, has been to express gratitude for the gifts I have received by teaching a curriculum, and by living a life, of grace.

2 Worlding Gifts, Grace and Gratitude

A Posthuman Pedagogy of Art, Affect and Belonging

Fiona Blaikie

Introduction

Embracing gratitude and worlding (Stewart, 2019), I curate a chronology of experiences, ideas, and people that stick with me emotionally (Ahmed, 2004), impacting my praxis as an artist, scholar and teacher.

Consider the situatedness of childhood habitus constructs (Bourdieu, 1984), wherein lives are pre-inscribed, enculturated, gendered, classed and affective. We live in collective thinking-feeling imaginaries:

> ...entangled in the worlds in which we move, from home to social settings to intimate relationships with ourselves and others, as well as places of work, study and recreation...As we move through our lives, across places, subcultures and times, via explicit and implicit codes for belonging, externalized through socially un/acceptable aesthetic codes and practices
>
> (Blaikie, 2018)

We engage constantly in worlding ourselves and others through storying. To begin worlding, I offer an image of a woman gazing at the Yamuna River in Agra, India:

The image of this woman sticks with me, yet, in asking "what do you see in this image?" others' responses are unique, entangled reworldings. Places and spaces in which we live affectively, relationally, in situated conditions, frame our early and ongoing habitus of being, becoming and belonging. My father Alexander wanted people to belong: "Be a gentle person who never embarrasses anyone" he said. His deep respect for the singular situated conditions of every life, human and nonhuman, has stayed with me.

DOI: 10.4324/9781003154112-3

Image 2.1 Photograph taken by Fiona Blaikie in April 2019 at Mehtab Bagh, Agra, India.

First Worlding (Storying): The Gift of Hermeneutic Phenomenology

As a masters student at the University of Victoria, Canada, in the lifechanging Summer of 1988, I took Foundations of Curriculum with visiting professor, Tom Barone (1983). Tom introduced Max van Manen's (1982) phenomenological pedagogy, intersecting scholarship, reflexivity, theory and practice via hermeneutic phenomenology, drawing on interpretations of meaning inherent in senses, experiences, feelings, words and images, and especially the vivacity of singular lived experiences. I met scholar Ted Aoki (1986): "I am honoured to speak with you, Dr. Aoki." "On the contrary" Ted said, "it is my honour to speak with you!" Gripped with enthusiasm, adopting a phenomenological approach to my thesis (Blaikie, 1989), I entered an unpredictable,

28   Fiona Blaikie

organically unfolding situated inquiry into art teachers' beliefs about art, teaching and curriculum, allowing for authentic respectful synergies between the particular and the universal in relation to questions such as: What is art? What does it mean to teach and learn art? How might we engage authentically in research and scholarship?

Second Worlding (Storying): Gifts of Engagements with Community/ies

Five years later I was completing my Ph.D., at the University of British Columbia (UBC) (Blaikie, 1992). Close to my dissertation defense, I was gifted with a tenure track position in art education at Lakehead University. I'm grateful to my supervisor, Ron MacGregor (1995), who urged me to take up the position. I drove my little blue car across Canada with my dog, Josie the Beast of Love. September 1, 1992: Josie and I woke up in a bleak motel on Arthur Street, Thunder Bay, feeling unmoored. At my new apartment that afternoon, with its popcorn ceilings and passages smelling of hot oil, sweat and bacon, movers started delivering furniture and boxes of books. "Please, stop! Take them back to the truck and back to Vancouver!" I crashed emotionally, irrationally pleading with George from Patullo Moving. "First off" he said, "do you have $2500 to pay for that, and does this new job have a dental plan and a pension?" "No, I don't, and yes, it does" I replied. "You've got to give it a year then" he said. I am grateful to George.

Living in Thunder Bay was life-giving. In 2000, with Janet Clark, Curator at Thunder Bay Art Gallery, we received a City of Thunder Bay Millennium Award to produce curriculum art kits, bringing local artists' work into classrooms. In 2002, working with the City of Thunder Bay's Arts and Heritage Committee, local school boards and arts organizations, and with Ontario Trillium funding, I created the Community Arts and Heritage Education Project (CAHEP) which continues today, supporting integrated community arts education programmes in schools, retirement homes and community centres (www.cahep.ca).

Third Worlding (Storying): Gifts of Porous Boundaries Connecting People, Theories and Ideas

In 2003, John Guiney Yallop was a doctoral student in the Joint Ph.D. Programme in Educational Studies. That year I became programme director. In my first Summer newsletter (Blaikie, 2004), I proudly announced publication of John's chapter (Guiney Yallop, 2004). Working together with John and other emerging scholars in the core 2 doctoral course, I was excited about my new pedagogical thematic approach to connecting the three fields of study: policy, leadership and admin'n; socio'l and political contexts; cognition and curriculum.

The overarching theme of the course was the ethics of care. This approach made disciplinary boundaries porous, enhancing connections between and across people and ideas. Our conversations were relevant and relational, and made space for surprises.

Serendipitously, a second gifting took place in 2006: I met Donal O'Donoghue (2007, 2018) at the International Society for Education through Art (INSEA) conference in Portugal. We discussed forms of arts-based research (Eisner, 1997), values inherent in materialities and aesthetics, leading me to arts-informed scholarship (Knowles and Cole, 2008). I began a new sustaining series of studies incorporating research-creation and social theory, looking at embodied, clothed, gendered, classed, enculturated, sexed and situated expressions and performances of scholars, youth and university students moving through shifting materializing identity constructs across time, place and space (Blaikie, 2007, 2009, 2012, 2013, 2018, 2020).

Fourth Worlding (Storying): Gifts of New Materialism, Affect Theory and Posthumanism

From 2010 to 2015, I served as Dean of the Faculty of Education at Brock University. When time permitted, my reading turned to new materialism and posthumanism, including Barad (2007), Coole and Frost (2010) and Bennett (2010). By 2015, I was ready to re-world myself as an artist-scholar-pedagogue.

Following Deleuze and Guattari (1987), I am drawn to the idea that we exist in collective states of immanence through the unfolding unpredictable present, drawing on natural instincts, where the sensing intuitive embodied self knows how to live, how to feel, how to imagine, and how to die. We do not need to be taught these things, just as a robin does not need to be taught how to build a nest for its eggs. Deleuze and Guattari's immanence is imagined as a condition of posthumanism (Barad, 2007; Blaikie, Daigle and Vasseur, 2020; Braidotti, 2019) because it speaks to relationalities, especially forces of nature. In posthumanism, humans are non-exceptional and simultaneously responsible for protecting our planet, humans and non-humans.

Many of us are shocked by ongoing destruction of our environment, and rampant cruelty to humans and nonhumans. When this impacts us directly, as Nochlin (1971) famously asserted, the personal is political.

Fifth Worlding (Storying): Gifts of Experiential Pedagogical Spaces and Places

The multiple material, affective, relational, enculturated settings in which we experience our lives and in which pedagogies unfold are themselves

Image 2.2 Photograph taken by Fiona Blaikie in April 2019 in Delhi, India.

little worldings: Living in the slum in the photograph above would be a particular inhabited experience of worlding, just as a family wedding and creating a home are worldings that are situated relationally, culturally, affectively and aesthetically in time and space: The spaces, objects and materialities in which we engage in pedagogy all *do* things, exercising an agentic capacity that inflects teaching and learning (Barad, 2007). Posthuman pedagogy asks us to create new ways of thinking-feeling by attuning ourselves, disrupting traditional ideas about classrooms as pedagogical spaces, and considering other spaces like the kitchen at home, or a nature walk.

The drawing below may trigger memories of a walk in the woods as an experiential pedagogical space of water, light, colour and ambiance. Pedagogy happens everywhere.

Sixth Worlding (Storying): Gifts of Ancestral Ways of Knowing

Being and becoming drawn into multimodal thinking-feeling beyond the intellect, into the instinctive, intuitive, affective "just knowing" part of ourselves is a gift. My maternal grandmother Mary grew up in genteel poverty in Edinburgh, Scotland. Her widowed mother raised three children. An orange at Christmas was a treat, and table manners were

Worlding Gifts, Grace and Gratitude 31

Image 2.3 Drawing by Fiona Blaikie, The Thames at Guildford, Surrey, 1981: Oil pastel on paper.

important. Granny spoke with a strong Scottish accent that got stronger after a "wee dram." She grew herbs and vegetables, and made bread, soap and candles. She was deeply attuned and knew things, like how our pet animals felt, what was going to happen, and what the weather was going to do. I am drawn to my Granny's praxis-oriented ancestral way of knowing, as well as Indigenous ways of knowing (Heckenberg, 2011) implicit in pedagogy as relational, situated and connected. Following Martin (2013), we don't own land, space and place. Rather, we belong to the land, to spaces and places.

Like ancestral ways of knowing, posthuman pedagogy asks us to attune to our unfolding being and becoming, drawing on instinct, affect and phenomenological lived experiences in scholarship, pedagogy and research (Blaikie, Daigle and Vasseur, 2020). For example, moving beyond a focus on teaching content, we might ask, how does a

32   *Fiona Blaikie*

traumatized child whose parents spent all night fighting make sense of grade three mathematics? How is mathematics relevant to her?

If, in worlding, we become attuned and connected to the present, in un-worlding we experience a frightening disconnect, outside of time and space, just as this fictional child might. Creating a sense of care and connection is key, requiring pedagogical presence and sensitivity to the nuances of shifting moments.

Seventh Worlding (Storying): Gifts of Holistic Pedagogies and Social-Justice via Scholarship as Narrative Research-Creation

During the 20th and 21st centuries, scholars, artists and teachers have made multiple efforts to create holistic pedagogies, for example, Maria Montessori, Rudolf Steiner and A.S. Neill's (1960) highly successful school *Summerhill*, "founded in 1921 and still ahead of its time" (http://www.summerhillschool.co.uk/an-overview.php). These efforts are connected to social justice encompassing the civil rights movement, second wave feminism, and an ethic of care and empowerment including Miller (1996), Freire (1970), hooks (1994), Noddings (1992) and Shields et al. (2011). Because of my social-justice oriented research creation work, I am drawn to scholarship on pedagogy in relation to class (Anyon, 1980), culture, race, gender and sexuality (Blaikie, 2007, 2009, 2012, 2013, 2018, 2020, 2021a, 2021b; O'Donoghue, 2007, 2018). These topics continue to be examined multi-modally, enhanced by the work of Aoki, Barone and Max van Manen who galvanized the move to narrative inquiry (Shields et al. 2011; Podolski, 2018), and arts-based research methods (Barone and Eisner, 2012; Knowles and Cole, 2008). Scholars working with art forms include the first novel as dissertation at UBC by Rishma Dunlop (1999), the poetry of Carl Leggo (2018), the poetry of John Guiney Yallop (2004, 2016), my own research-creation (Blaikie, 2007, 2009, 2013, 2018, 2020), and important participatory emancipatory post-qualitative research (Lather and St. Pierre, 2013).

Research-creation work supporting holistic pedagogies and social justice themes moving toward post-disciplinarity (Darbellay, 2020) is key to disciplines taught via porous entanglements, complexities and intricacies, fostering capacities to experiment, explore and discover. A theme such as "space" across arts and science disciplines allows for deep, broad, holistic system wide feeling and thinking to develop. In the painting below of pears in space, I was thinking about relationality, space, and a moment in time and context. As creators and participants, in reading poetry, listening to music and looking at art, we feel, remember and imagine, drawing on individual and collective imaginaries. I asked my partner to tell me about this painting of pears:

Image 2.4 Painting by Fiona Blaikie, Space, 2015: Oils on canvas.

> The pears are gilded by light, made material and artifactual. They are on a surface, but not located. Both of and not of their space – they appear to float up out of it. The reclining pear on the left is resting, fallen perhaps, but the light shines through it, giving it a sense of weightlessness and peace.
> (Personal communication, July 20, 2020)

Conclusion: Worlding Gifts, Grace and Gratitude

I am grateful to Carmen, Adam and John for inviting me to frame a worlding praxis of experiences, ideas and people that continue to stick with me emotionally (Ahmed, 2004), impacting my life as a practising artist, scholar and teacher. I am grateful to scholars whose work is inspirational, along with my valued colleagues, students, family and friends, and the serendipitous kindness of strangers over the years, like George from Patullo Moving.

Drawing on Bourdieusian (1984) habitus, I followed Stewart's (2019) worlding, offering storied vignettes featuring hermeneutic phenomenology; serendipitous opportunities for work and community engagement; porous connections with people and ideas across disciplines; new materialism, affect theory and posthumanism; experiential pedagogical spaces; ancestral ways of knowing and holistic pedagogies, and social

34 *Fiona Blaikie*

justice via scholarship as narrative research-creation. In my posthuman pedagogy, humans recognize their non-exceptionality and responsibility to live in concert with nonhumans and the environment. They attune sensitively to issues of difference and inherent connectedness through materialities and relationalities across worldings of spaces and places, in and through ancestral ways of knowing, privileging affect, connections, and belonging, recognizing gifts, grace, and gratitude.

References

Ahmed, S. (2004). *The Cultural Politics of Emotion*. Croydon: Routledge.

Anyon, J. (1980). The Hidden Curriculum of Work. *Journal of Education, 162*, (1). 1–6. http://www1.udel.edu/educ/whitson/897s05/files/hiddencurriculum.html

Aoki, T. et al. (1986). *Understanding curriculum as lived: Curriculum Canada VI*. Vancouver: University of British Columbia.

Barad, K. (2007). *Meeting the Universe Halfway: Quantum Physics and the Entanglement of Matter and Meaning*. London: Duke University Press.

Barone, T. (1983). Education as aesthetic experience: Art in germ. *Educational Leadership, 40*(4), 21–27.

Barone, T., & Eisner, E. (2012). *Arts Based Research*. Los Angeles, CA: Sage.

Bennett, J. (2010). *Vibrant Matter: A Political Ecology of Things*. Durham, NC: Duke University Press.

Blaikie, F. (2021a). Introduction. In F. Blaikie (Ed.). *Visual and Cultural Identity Constructs of Global Youth and Young Adults*. (pp. 1–18). Routledge. https://www.routledge.com/Visual-and-Cultural-Identity-Constructs-of-Global-Youth-Situated-Embodied/Blaikie/p/book/9780367519490

Blaikie, F. (2021b). Worlding youth: visual and narrative vignettes embodying being, becoming, and belonging. In F. Blaikie (Ed.). *Visual and Cultural Identity Constructs of Global Youth and Young Adults*. (pp. 36–61). Routledge. https://www.routledge.com/Visual-and-Cultural-Identity-Constructs-of-Global-Youth-Situated-Embodied/Blaikie/p/book/9780367519490

Blaikie, F., Daigle, C., & Vasseur, L. (2020). *Posthumanism and Education: New Approaches*. The CCUNESCO Idea Lab. Ottawa, Canada.

Blaikie, F. (2020). Worlding Danny: Being, Becoming, and Belonging. *Studies in Art Education: A Journal of Issues and Research, 61*(4), 330–348. DOI: 10.1080/00393541.2020.1820831

Blaikie, F. (2018). Habitus, Visual and Cultural Identity: Mean Girls' Hyperfeminine Performances as Burlesque Pastiche and as Archetypal Female Pariahs, *Studies in Art Education, 59* (3), 15–227. DOI: 10.1080/00393541.2018.1476951

Blaikie, F. (2013). Navigating Conversion: An Arts-Based Inquiry into the Clothed Body and Identity. *The Journal of Visual Culture and Gender, 8*. 57–69.

Blaikie, F. (2012). A poetic and visual inquiry into the male professoriate: Clive, Todd, Mark and William. *In the Canadian Review of Art Education: Issues and Research, 38*, 45–67.

Blaikie, F. (2009). Knowing Bodies: A Visual and Poetic Inquiry into the Professoriate. *International Journal of Education and the Arts*. http://www.ijea.org/v10n8/index.html

Worlding Gifts, Grace and Gratitude 35

Blaikie, F. (2007). The Aesthetics of Female Scholarship: Rebecca, Kris, Paula and Lisette. *Journal of the Canadian Association for Curriculum Studies*. http://www.csse.ca/CACS/JCACS/V5N2/PDFContent/00.%20intro.pdf

Blaikie, F. (2004). Joint Ph.D. in Educational Studies Newsletter. Joint Ph.D. in Educational Studies Program. https://jointphd-ed.lakeheadu.ca/wp-content/uploads/2019/12/Newsletter-2004-Fall.pdf Accessed July 20th 2020.

Blaikie, F. (1992). *Structures of and aesthetic values inherent in senior secondary studentassessment in studio art in Britain and North America: International Baccalaureate, Advanced Placement, General Certificate in Secondary Education (UK) and Arts Propel (USA)*. Vancouver, BC: University of British Columbia, Ph.D. dissertation. Supervisor: Dr. Ron MacGregor.

Blaikie, F. (1989). *Beliefs of secondary art teachers in relation to educational backgrounds, curricular issues and teaching practices*. Victoria, BC: University of Victoria., MA thesis. Supervisor: Dr William Zuk

Braidotti, R. (2019). *Posthuman Knowledge*. Cambridge, UK: Polity Press.

Bourdieu, P. (1984). *Distinction: A social critique of the judgment of taste*. Cambridge, MA: Harvard University Press.

Coole, D., & Frost, S. (Eds.). (2010). *New Materialisms: Ontology, Agency, Politics*. Durham, NC: Duke University Press.

Darbellay, F. (2020). Postdisciplinarity: imagine the future, think the unthinkable. In Barone, T. & Pernecky, T. (Ed.). *Postdisciplinary Knowledge*. (pp. 235–250). London: Routledge.

Deleuze, G., & Guattari, F. (1987). *A Thousand Plateaus: Capitalism and Schizophrenia* (Trans, B. Massumi.) Minneapolis, MN: Minnesota Press.

Dunlop, R. (1999). *Boundary Bay: A novel as educational research*. University of British Columbia: Doctoral Dissertation. ProQuest Dissertations Publishing.

Eisner, E. W. (1997). The Promise and Perils of Alternative Forms of Data Representation. *Educational researcher, 26*(6), 4– 10.

Freire, P. (1970). *Pedagogy of the Oppressed*. New York: Seabury Press.

Guiney Yallop, J. (2016). *Out of Place*. Victoria, BC: Friesen.

Guiney Yallop, J. (2004). Gay and Out in Secondary School: One Youth's Story. In J. McNinch and M. Cronin (Eds.), *I Could Not Speak My Heart: Education and Social Justice for Gay and Lesbian Youth* (pp. 29–42). Regina: Canadian Plains Research Center.

Heckenberg, R. (2011). Holding heart: Aboriginal breathing space in research epistemology. *International Journal of Interdisciplinary Social Sciences, 5*(9), 107– 118.

hooks, bb. (1994). *Teaching to transgress*. New York, NY: Routledge.

Knowles, J., & Cole, A. (2008). *Handbook of the arts in qualitative research: Perspectives, methodologies, examples, and issues*. Los Angeles: Sage.

Lather, P., & St. Pierre, E. (2013). Post-qualitative research. *International Journal of Qualitative Studies in Education, 26* (6). 629–633. DOI: 10.1080/0951839 8.2013.788752

Leggo, C. (2018). Poetry in the Academy: A Language of Possibility. *Canadian Journal of Education, 41*(1), 69– 97.

MacGregor, R. (1995). Etcetera. *Art Education: ...And Now, on Several Other Matters, 48*(6), 5–5. https://doi.org/10.1080/00043125.1995.11652356 accessed on July 20th 2020.

36 Fiona Blaikie

Martin, B. (2013). Immaterial Land. In Bolt, B. and Barrett, E. (Eds.). *Carnal Knowledge: Towards a New Materialism through the Arts*. (pp. 185–204). London: IB Tauris.

Miller, J. P. (1996). *The Holistic Curriculum*. Toronto: OISE Press.

Neill, A. S. (1960). *Summerhill*. New York: Hart.

Noddings, N. (1992). *The challenge to care in schools: An alternative approach to education*. New York: Teachers College Press.

Nochlin, L. (1971). Why have there been no great women artists? In Gornick, V. and Moran, B. (Eds.). *Woman in sexist society: Studies in power and powerlessness*. (pp. 480–510). New York: Basic Books.

O'Donoghue, D. (2018). *Learning to Live in Boys' Schools: Art-led Understandings of Masculinities*. New York: Routledge.

O'Donoghue, D. (2007). "James always hangs out here": Making space for place in studying masculinities at school. *Visual Studies*, 22(1), 62–73. doi:10.1080/14725860601167218

Podolski, A. G. (2018). *Towards a personal philosophy of curriculum, approaching currere and narrative inquiry within an aokian paradigm of reciprocity*. Nipissing University: Doctoral Dissertation. http://hdl.handle.net/1807/92715

Shields, C., Novak, N., Marshall, B., & Yallop, J. (2011). Providing visions of a different life: Self-study narrative inquiry as an instrument for seeing ourselves in previously-unimagined places. *Narrative Works*, 1(1), 63–77.

Stewart, K. (2019). Granite. Correspondences, *Fieldsights*. https://culanth.org/fieldsights/granite Accessed February 19th 2020.

Van Manen, M. (1982) Phenomenological Pedagogy. *Curriculum Inquiry*, 12 (3). 283–299. DOI: 10.1080/03626784.1982.11075844 Accessed July 20th 2020.

3 The Way of Gratitude

Ashwani Kumar

The Way of Gratitude
Is the way of humility, grace, and gratefulness.
The Way of Gratitude
Is the way to be happy, content, and blissful.
The Way of Gratitude
Is the way of peace, friendship, and prayer.
The Way of Gratitude
Is the way of love, trust, and compassion.
The Way of Gratitude
Is the way of meditation, awareness, and wholeness.
The Way of Gratitude is the Way to Be.

I am thankful for this chance to share what I am grateful for as a curriculum theorist, a teacher educator, and a human being. This is a rare opportunity as in the academic world we are often expected to talk about our accomplishments, achievements, impacts, and so on but we are hardly ever asked to share what we are grateful for, who has contributed to our lives and work, to our journeys. Often, expressions of gratitude are hidden away in the acknowledgments in books and theses. In my writings, however, guided by Bill Pinar's notion of *currere* and autobiographical inquiry (Pinar, 2012), I have tried to challenge this limitation and have often acknowledged those who have contributed to my ideas and practices and how they have done so (see Kumar, 2013, 2014, 2019; Kumar & Downey, 2018a, 2019).

I see this exceptional opportunity of expressing our gratitude as an invitation to challenge the ego-centric, male-dominant, colonial, and capitalistic academic paradigm. I consider this to be a beautiful occasion to be grateful and graceful, heartful and thankful, prayerful and hopeful, creative and meditative.

It is a tremendous occasion to share what/who have been our inspirations and influences, guides and supports, mentors and teachers. We are not isolated, ego-driven, and ego-centric entities as we are often reduced to in our capitalistic and individualistic world driven by competition

DOI: 10.4324/9781003154112-4

38 Ashwani Kumar

and comparison. To be is to be related. To exist implies coexistence. And therefore, to live is to be grateful to other beings without whom we cannot exist. It is important to reflect on and be grateful to those who have been responsible for our arising, those with whom we have been related to (knowingly and unknowingly), and those who teach us and learn from us.

I Am Grateful

I am grateful
To the never-ending, mysterious, and unfathomable Existence –
    the unknowable source of creativity and *everybeing* that exists
To Mother Earth which is the ground of our arising
To Sun whose energy sustains life on Earth
To Great Nature for its Marvellous Order and Harmony
To the beautiful Lands, Trees, and Waters without which life will not
    be possible
To the Air, the Life Force, that we breathe
To All Sentient Beings for sharing their lives

I am grateful
To my parents who brought me to this world
To my mother who bore all the pains to raise me and my siblings
To my father for his interest in religion and philosophy
To my wife for her love, patience, trust, and care
To my siblings for being there
To my nieces for their childhood and all the beauty that comes with it
To my friends ... friends are the salt of the earth ... how I miss my
    friends from India

I am grateful to India – the place of my birth, upbringing, and education –
For its Great Culture
For giving to the world Yoga, Ayurveda, and Raag Music
For its spiritual way of life
For its revered and true teachers and to its dedicated students
For its innumerable languages, regions, cultures, and ways of being
For its colourful, mysterious, and mind-blowing mythologies and literatures
For its rivers and seas, for the Indian Ocean and the Great Himalayas
For an unending variety of vegetarian delicacies
For the sense of informality, friendliness, and spontaneity among its
    people
For the absence of crystalized egos and their suffocating isolation

I am grateful to Canada – the place where I live and work –
For its Indigenous Cultures, Knowledges, and Ways of Being

The Way of Gratitude   39

For its enchanting beauty and diversity
> How lucky I was to live on the UBC campus in Vancouver for four years!
> How lucky I am to live in Mi'kma'ki (Nova Scotia) and work at MSVU!

For its open-heartedness and acceptance
For respecting my individuality, my ideas
For helping me realize my dream to be a professor
For giving me some amazing teachers, friends, and colleagues
For even creating the space where I could learn yoga, raag music, and
  about Ayurveda!

I am grateful to all my teachers
Without whom I would not be what I am
For their generosities, care, and deep affection
For their selfless dedication
For their deep knowledge, their ability to share without withholding
For their engagement, for sharing a dialogue, for igniting a sense of
  never-ending inquiry
For their commitment to creating a world full of creative,
  compassionate, and meditative people
For their emphasis on the way of meditative inquiry

I am grateful to my students
For learning from me and with me and for teaching me
For letting me share my educational experiences and sharing their own
  with me
For their openness, curiosity, courage, and love of learning
For their desire for understanding and for their faith in change
For challenging the ardent and widespread belief in testing,
  comparison, and competition
For working together for an education that respects students' freedom
  and creative expression
For engaging with me and their students in authentic and
  transformative dialogue
For engaging with meditative inquiry and letting it flower and mature

I am grateful to raag music
For its meditative melodiousness
For its tenderness and subtlety
For the possibility of improvisation
For creating a state of being where musician disappears but music
  stays
For being my path to creativity – the essence of existence
For helping me discover within myself the art of composition
For giving me the opportunity to compose – something that is as
  natural to me as breathing

40 *Ashwani Kumar*

For giving voice to my feelings and emotions, dilemmas and conflicts, suffering and turmoil
For allowing me to be devotional without undermining the significance of critique
For connecting me to the beauty of the culture of India at a deeper level
For creating opportunities to listen to other artists and teachers and learn from them

I am grateful.

Who Am I?

Like curriculum, self is a complex and complicated, rich and varied, unique and creative being. I am a person related to other persons and sentient beings, to the earth, to the sky, and to the whole of this beautiful and extraordinary existence.

I am an Indian and a Canadian
I am a son, a husband, a brother, an uncle, a nephew, a teacher, a student, and a friend
I am a singer, a composer, and a poet
I am a curriculum theorist, a holistic educator, a philosopher, and a geographer.
All the multiple expressions and constitutions of my self are indebted to and are grateful for their arising, existence, and growth.
I am grateful.
And yet,
I am also a meditator
But "I" or "the meditator" cannot exist in meditation!
This is not a semantic, but an existential issue.
Meditative awareness opens the door to what lies beyond the limitations of self
Or, meditative awareness lies beyond the sense of "I" and its intricacies.

A Narrative of Gratitude

In Hindi, my first language, there is a famous phrase called "Gagar Mein Sagar." It literally means "Ocean in a Pot." Metaphorically, it means conveying what you want to convey in as few words as you can. That is perhaps the reason why ancient Indian philosophers and mystics chose to express their thoughts in poetry, mantras, and sutras. While pages can be written to expand on what I have tried to convey in my poetic reflections, and while I am afraid that my prose will not do justice to what I want to say, I feel that there is a need to include a short narrative of gratitude to provide the context to what I have shared above.

While unconsciously and subconsciously I have been deeply influenced by my parents and elders, my upbringing and education, and the culture

The Way of Gratitude 41

of India, the first conscious influence on me that I consider immensely profound was Kabir – a mystic and poet from medieval India (for documentaries and other material on Kabir see the "Kabir Project" online). I read him for the first time when I was in grade nine. His poetry was part of the Hindi curriculum. I still remember one verse that left a strong impression on me and alerted me to the dangers of organized religions and their superstitions and made me aware of what it means to be truly spiritual.

> I do not know what manner of God is mine.
> The Mullah cries aloud to Him: and why? Is your Lord deaf? The subtle anklets that ring on the feet of an insect when it moves are heard of Him.
> Tell your beads, paint your forehead with the mark of your God, and wear matted locks long and showy: but a deadly weapon is in your heart, and how shall you have God?
> (Kabir in Tagore, 1915, pp. 110–111)

His work laid the foundations of a spiritual life that continued to evolve throughout my youth and brought me to the work of Osho – a highly knowledgeable and yet very controversial teacher from India who has produced hundreds of commentaries on spiritual and literary texts from all over the world including several on the poetry of Kabir. I spent many years of my life seriously reading and discussing his works and experimenting with his meditations. Despite all the controversies, and despite my own questioning, I find him to be one of the most knowledgeable, provocative, and creative persons I have studied and who has deeply informed the way I engage with life. His works also introduced me to many literary figures, philosophers, and mystics including J. Krishnamurti and George Gurdjieff – two of the most revolutionary teachers of the twentieth century. Kabir, Osho, Krishnamurti, Gurdjieff, and my friend Ashutosh Kalsi, who I met in Vancouver, together have deeply influenced my life as well as my work in academia. Engaging and experimenting with their ideas allowed me to realize the significance of understanding and transforming human consciousness that is at the very source of our social, political, economic, and educational structures and their problems. My personal and academic engagement with the study of consciousness has helped me to share four interrelated theoretical and practical educational concepts with my colleagues and students, namely, *curriculum as meditative inquiry* (Kumar, 2013), *teaching as meditative inquiry* (Kumar & Downey, 2018a; Kumar & Acharya, 2021), *music as meditative inquiry* (Kumar & Downey, 2019), and *dialogical meditative inquiry* (Kumar & Downey, 2018a, 2018b, 2019). An edited collection of scholarly writings – *Engaging with Meditative Inquiry in Teaching, Learning, and Research: Realizing Transformative Potentials in Diverse*

42 Ashwani Kumar

Contexts – that engage with my work on meditative inquiry is in its final stages as I write this chapter. I am grateful for the consideration of my ideas by my colleagues and students.

My academic and intellectual journey more or less coincided with my spiritual journey, and it truly began when I started my undergraduate studies in geography at Kirori Mal College (KMC) of the University of Delhi and met the late Professor K.K. Mojumdar. I am deeply, very deeply grateful that I met this man. Going to KMC was in some ways revolutionary for me. Having grown up in a disadvantaged single parent family (it was unheard of and is still not that common in India) and having studied in Hindi medium and deficient government schools at the rural outskirts of New Delhi, it was a culture shock for me to be suddenly in one of the most reputed colleges of the University of Delhi amidst middle-class English-speaking students and teachers. Luckily, there were some other students who shared my socio-economic background, and, to our great fortune, we had two professors, Professors Mojumdar and Kaushal Kumar Sharma, who extended their support to us. Their kindness, sensitivity to our disadvantaged upbringing, and unwavering support gave me and others the confidence to be where we are now. Professor Mojumdar was perhaps the most knowledgeable and most widely read individual I have ever met in my life. And to my great fortune, I learned from him, one-on-one, for about a decade and almost on a daily basis, during my eight-year-long studies in geography (B.A., M.A., and M.Phil.) and three-year-long studies in education (B.Ed. and M.Ed.). Just being with him, through spontaneous dialogues, I imbibed what it means to be an academic in the true sense of the word rather than what it has become in the neoliberal capitalist world. I am sorry that he is no more. He had a stroke when I was about to leave for Canada, and he did not live long after that. Being with him and his wife in the hospital is one of the toughest experiences I have gone through but something that taught me that there is no bigger virtue than being grateful to those who contributed to your life selflessly.

The trajectory of my academic life brought me to the discipline of education and led me to pursue a Ph.D. in curriculum studies at the University of British Columbia in 2007. How fortunate I am that there I met another significant mentor, Bill Pinar, who, needless to say, has been a mentor not only to countless other students and scholars, but to the field of curriculum studies itself. His love of autobiography and complicated conversation deeply influenced and inspired my personality, my teaching, and my research. Without his support and affection, I would not be where I am presently and would not have been able to accomplish what I have. Besides Professors Majoumdar and Pinar, there have been many other teachers who supported me in India and Canada including Professors Kaushal Kumar Sharma, Rama Mathew, Shyam Menon, Anne Phelan, Anthony Clarke, Karen Meyer, and E. Wayne

Ross, among others. My deepest gratitude to all of them and to the discipline of geography and curriculum theory for their interdisciplinary character and openness to diverse perspectives and forms of expression.

My life would have remained incomplete if I had not pursued my interest in Indian classical music or raag music. A raag is melodious flow that permeates you deeply, evokes deep emotions and sensations, and brings about a meditative vitality in your being. While I have always been interested in music, particularly old Bollywood classics and ghazal music (ghazal is a form of Urdu poetry), and while I always had the desire to learn music, my socio-economic family background, deficient school resources, and lack of time never allowed me to learn music. While in my Ph.D. program at UBC, and in the beautiful ambience of its campus, an interest in learning music began to stir in me, but for one reason or the other I could not formally start my musical journey with a teacher. Interestingly, I did learn yoga in Vancouver, thanks to my friend Hannah Spector. When I moved to Halifax, my thirst to learn music became more intense, and in 2013 I found a teacher of Indian classical music, Mr. Vijay Vyas. I also started learning from my uncle, Mr. M.C. Gotan, in India soon after. Nobody has supported me in music and cared for my growth in music as my uncle has. I am very, very grateful to him. I am not sure if I have learned anything so deeply and so passionately as I have raag music. And given the number of songs and tunes I have composed over the years, I am not sure if I have ever been as creative and "productive" – how I hate this word! – either. Music for me is meditation and music as meditative inquiry is their unified expression. I am grateful, very grateful that I have experienced raag music in my life. And I am lucky, very lucky that I met my wife, also a student of raag music, in a music class.

I am grateful, very grateful
For life has given me more than I deserve
For I have experienced creativity, love, and moments of meditativeness
For I have no regrets.

References

Kumar, A. (2013). *Curriculum as meditative inquiry*. New York: Palgrave Macmillan.

Kumar, A. (2014). Meditative education: A proposal for the existential renewal of teacher education in the 21st century. In M. J. Harkins & Z. Barchuk (Eds.), *Conversations with international teacher educators: Teaching in a global world* (pp. 95–116, e-Book). Halifax: Faculty of Education, Mount Saint Vincent University. Available online at: http://www.msvu.ca/site/media/msvu/Documents/E-Book%20International%20Conversations%20of%20Teacher%20Educators%20Teaching%20and%20Learning%20in%20Global%20World%281%29.pdf.

44 Ashwani Kumar

Kumar, A. (2019). *Curriculum in international contexts: Understanding colonial, ideological and neoliberal influences*. New York, NY: Palgrave Macmillan.

Kumar, A., & Acharya, N. (2021). Critiquing instrumentalism in higher education: Lessons from teaching as meditative inquiry. *Critical Education, 12*(10), 1–23. https://ices.library.ubc.ca/index.php/criticaled/article/view/186628

Kumar, A., & Downey, A. (2018a). Teaching as meditative inquiry: A dialogical exploration. *Journal of the Canadian Association for Curriculum Studies, 16*(2), 52–75. https://jcacs.journals.yorku.ca/index.php/jcacs/article/view/40339/36397.

Kumar, A. & Downey, A. (2018b). *Dialogical meditative inquiry: An existential and emergent approach to research. Presentation at The 35th Annual Qualitative Analysis Conference*, St. Thomas University, Fredericton, NB.

Kumar, A., & Downey, A. (2019). Music as meditative inquiry: Dialogical reflections on learning and composing Indian classical music. *Artizein: Arts and Teaching Journal, 4*(2), 98–121. https://opensiuc.lib.siu.edu/atj/vol4/iss1/9/

Pinar, W. (2012). *What is curriculum theory?* (2nd ed.). New York: Routledge.

Tagore, R. (Trans.). (1915). *Songs of Kabir*. New York, NJ: The Macmillan.

4 When Curriculum Disrupts

A Case for Gratitude After Decades of Being Surprised

Carmen Schlamb

I remember thinking when I was a student that there was little that surprised me. With the brazen attitude of youth (that I can only admire now several decades later as a time of life on *full throttle*), I had meticulously planned my pathway forward – choosing the "right" school and academic program, performing part-time work I thought would translate well on a resume and even dedicating my leisure time to the ultimate goal of *making it* in my chosen field.

Surprises, I believed, were what you received when your planning efforts had failed. In my mind, chance and circumstance had no place in a well-developed plan and life, and so anything outside my defined parameters for success were considered temporary disruptions, mere spokes in my wheel that had to be fixed before moving forward.

When I was invited to contribute to this collection, with its focus on gratitude and gifts in curriculum studies, this memory of my earlier self is what first came to mind. Interestingly enough, it wasn't a particular place, person, or event that I was most grateful for when considering all that I had learned in this field of education; rather, it seemed I was more drawn to the commonality that seemed to bind all my grateful experiences together – the formidable force of disruption followed closely by the element of surprise.

It is important in this telling to note that today I live and "think narratively" (Murphy, Huber & Clandinin, 2012, p. 231), that I have come to understand that my own learning stems from both the stories I experience and the ones I tell in hopes of gaining a whole view (Atkinson, 1995). It wasn't always this way for me (Schlamb, 2017), and I initially struggled with the idea that "all narratives are essentially incomplete" (Baldwin, 2011, p. 106) and are "co-authored" either directly or indirectly by our lived experiences to forever transform and change the way we see the world and our place in it (Mishler, 1995, p. 117).

Sometimes, when you live and work narratively, clarity can come from some of the most unexpected sources and experiences may come to have meaning long after they have passed. This is what Clandinin & Connelly (1994) refer to as the process of inward, outward, backward, forward reflection.

DOI: 10.4324/9781003154112-5

I am not usually an avid consumer of pop culture, but when thinking back on my educational journey for this writing I remembered an episode I had seen of HBO's hit comedy series *Silicon Valley* when I was introduced to the use of the word *disrupt* in relation to the technology field. In the show, a small but diligent group of young computer programmers plan to reveal their innovative algorithm at the annual TechCrunch Disrupt conference (HBO, 2020), a real life Silicon Valley event that features "five days of non-stop online programming" meant to "[shape] the future of disruptive technology and ideas" (Verizon Media, 2020, para. 1).

Apart from the witty dialogue and comedic timing of the script, the episode had captivated me with its reference to "disruptive technology" which Smith (2020) defines as "innovation that significantly alters the way that consumers, industries, or businesses operate" (para. 1). I was intrigued with the IT sector's intentional pursuit of disruption, an act that often carries a more menacing connotation and comes from the Latin *disruptus* meaning "to break apart," "to throw into disorder," and to "interrupt the normal course or unity" (Merriam-Webster, 2020).

With this reference in mind, I researched the idea of intentional disruption further and found a fascinating business theory based on the Disruption Innovation Model which highlights why "a smaller company with fewer resources is able to successfully challenge established incumbent businesses" (Christensen, Raynor, & McDonald, 2015, para. 6), or essentially shake up the status quo. In this theory, businesses that focus on prioritizing "sustaining innovations" also "inadvertently [starve] disruptive innovations" (para. 34) that might lead to positive change.

My limited research into these fields left me with much to think about in my own field of curriculum studies. Had disruption ever played a positive role in my teaching and learning? Had I ever purposefully sought disruption as a way of upsetting my own status quo? Had I inadvertently starved myself of opportunities that would have challenged my own incumbency?

To understand these questions more fully, I leaned into narrative inquiry, self-study with the belief that to know my self better is to know education better (Pinar, 1994; Bullough & Pinnegar 2001). Through deep reflection, I came to see my curriculum journey as a series of starts and stops over the past four decades – a plan derailed, the meeting of a mentor with the same name, and a push towards higher education that became a pull toward teaching and living narratively.

By adopting a holistic view, I was able to see these starts and stops as permanent landmarks on my identity landscape (Schlamb, 2017), when two roads did not necessarily diverge in a yellow wood (Frost, 2020/1915), but more accurately, when entire forests were in danger of clear-cut. While these recognizable moments vary in their place, space

When Curriculum Disrupts   47

and time, one constant that connects them all is how inspiration and influence came to me in the form of disruption and left me in surprise and with gratitude.

Disruption #1: A Plan Derailed

Sometimes all the signs are there but for some reason we just cannot see them. This sentiment best describes my feelings regarding my early post-secondary journey when I entered university for the first time armed with a take-no-prisoners attitude, and exited four months later in what can most accurately be called a shame-filled retreat with a handful of mediocre grades as my spoils.

What had happened to the well-developed plan that had prepared me for post-secondary learning? Where had my confidence gone?

In truth, I was in the wrong place and the curriculum I had anxiously anticipated had not spoken to me. Looking back as Pinar (2012) suggests to "undertake...social and subjective reconstruction," utilizing past and future lenses "however unpleasant each domain may prove to be" (p. 5), I can see clearly now that while I had done well academically prior to university, my heart had never been truly dedicated to what I had imagined my future career would be.

My decision to leave university in that first year resulted in a disruption of maximum proportions. Everything that had been planned over the years was gone, and more importantly everything I had believed about how to be in this life had to be reimagined as I moved from a place of certainty to a place of "becoming" within a "context that also is always becoming" (Kilgore, 2004, p. 47). As Aoki (1990) suggests, I had to rethink what it meant to "excel" and to come to a "deeper understanding" of what it meant to "[surpass my] present being" (p. 111).

The following year I found new direction in an unexpected but authentic place that resided in my margins of unpredictability (Edgerton, 2010), and I was surprised with how easy it was to learn, engage and find my way "*into* the world" (Pinar, 2012, p. xv, original emphasis) with new curriculum of my own making. Looking back on that period of time, I am grateful for the uninvited disruption that awoke me to finding *my right place*, and for introducing me to what can only be called "the art of curriculum" (Doll, 1993, p. 117) that engaged me in its most meaningful form and spoke to my head while simultaneously speaking to my heart.

Disruption #2: A Mentor of the Same Name

The path to my current teaching position that I hold at the post-secondary level has been anything but conventional. Somewhere after leaving university in that first year I became greatly engaged and utterly committed to education. When a commitment is made, at least in my case, it is

48   Carmen Schlamb

hard to pull back on the reins once the horses have been set free. So it was in my early teaching career, when full of ideas and energy, that I encountered what I considered to be another roadblock in my movement forward to meaningful life's work.

It was suggested to me that it might be in my best interests to pursue graduate school if I was interested in making education my career. I responded to the suggestion with a less than enthusiastic grunt citing multiple examples of education I had already taken that "had led me nowhere." Frustrated at the time with what I considered largely to be jumping through hoops, I enrolled in graduate school and flipped through the course offerings for the fall start-up that back then were mostly taught in person.

It might make some people smile when they hear the honesty with which I shall confess what I did next. So uninvested was I in the process before me (that I believed was none of my choosing) that I picked my first graduate level course according to the professor's name. Listed among what I would come to know over the next nine years as highly engaged and insightful scholars, I saw a professor's name that was the same as mine – "Carmen," and signed up for her leadership in mentoring course. My thought back then was simply "how bad could she be with a name like that?"

On our first evening of class, music was playing as I entered the classroom. "Ok, that's nice" I thought, and I found a spot in the circle of chairs facing inwards. When everyone was seated, Dr. Carmen Shields opened a book, one from the many she had stacked on the side table, and began reading a passage aloud about the process of becoming, her voice soft and lyrical, taking her time like all we had was that moment to share. She stood up and walked to the blackboard where she wrote "life is curriculum" and then sat slowly back down. She turned to the group then and said "in the field of educational leadership and curriculum, your stories matter. What story would you like to share today about your journey here?"

Later in my career, I would model her effective teaching techniques "such as slowing down, offering respectful silence, modeling caring and sharing in the rich dialogue of inquiry [that] are critical elements of our teaching and therapeutic practice" but it was her clear dedication to the act of kindness that opened an "emergent learning space" (Shields & Reid-Patton, 2009, p. 5) for me and for others in the class.

Now, 13 years have gone by and I still think about that evening when I was first told my stories mattered. I consider Carmen and that class to have been one of the greatest disruptions to my life to date. What she said about stories jarred my sense of order, challenging everything I had learned up to that point of what it meant to be *teacher*, what it meant to be *student*, and what *curriculum* could be, but had never been. I was surprised in the weeks that followed that first class how freely the stories came to me, and I am still surprised today that they haven't stopped

When Curriculum Disrupts 49

coming. Grateful is too small a word to relay how life changing that moment was and would be as I moved forward in my career and life.

The Disruption Continues: A Life Demanding to Be Lived Narratively

What originated as a push towards graduate school as part of building a hopeful career in education, has evolved into an undeniable pull towards living and working narratively. Looking backwards through the years, I can see my life has been full of disruptions, big and small, some recognizable for what they were and some more hidden in their impact. I have learned to sort these memories using story, interpreting them to make meaning in my life and work. This process allows me to see "contradictions within the self," exposing my ignorance (Feuerstein, Gonzalez, Porten, & Valens, 2014, p. xi) and essentially shedding a light on why I am surprised by the result of things. These moments of clarity remind me to embrace the *surprise of otherness* itself (Johnson, 2014) which celebrates and "recognize[s] the transformative power of truly experiencing our doubt, which can change the nature of what we thought we knew" (Feuerstein, Gonzalez, Porten, & Valens, 2014, p. xi). Upon completing this writing, I have come to understand that there is no learning without some form of disruption. How the disruption is embraced becomes the surprise. If all of life is curriculum, then I can say with confidence that curriculum, and those that continue to share and surprise me with it, are what I am most grateful for in this journey.

Not all disruption has to be massive for it to be meaningful. Through retrospection, I can recall small, quiet moments in time that gently agitated the sustaining existence I had created and relied upon, like small ripples in an otherwise still pond. Today, I cannot say with confidence that I intentionally invite disruption in, only that I now leave a previously bolted door unlocked, and have set an extra place at the table if it decides it would like to stay.

I wish to pay forward all that has been gifted to me through curriculum and its caregivers – the scholars of the past, the disruptors of the present, and the students of the future who may choose to enrol in my class because it fits their schedule or because they like the sound of my name. It is because of them that I now have the ability to celebrate the chaos that comes from the unexpected journey and to find gratitude in the act of being surprised. For them, I will dedicate myself to being the ripple in the water, the voice that challenges and disrupts at the front of the room, and the ear that listens when the stories come...as they surely will. I wish to eventually see what Palmer (2018) sees on the "brink of everything," a life that "has been graced" but has not necessarily "been graceful" (p. ix) and to "grow old and die in the same way [I've] lived [my life]" (p. ix). If all of this can be achieved, then I shall be profoundly grateful!

References

Aoki, T. (1990). Beyond the half-life of curriculum and pedagogy. *delta-K, 28*(2), 5–12.

Atkinson, R. (1995). *Gift of stories: Practical and spiritual applications of autobiography, life stories, and personal mythmaking.* Bergin & Garvey. Westport, Connecticut

Baldwin, C. (2011). *Living narratively: From theory to experience (and back again).* A presentation at the fourth annual John McKendy Memorial Lecture on Narrative at St. Thomas University, Fredericton, NB.

Bullough, R. V., & Pinnegar, S. (2001). Guidelines for quality in autobiographical forms of self-study research. *Educational Researcher, 30*(3), 13–21.

Christensen, C. M., Raynor, M. E., & McDonald, R. (December 2015). What is disruptive innovation? *Harvard Business Review.* https://hbr.org/2015/12/what-is-disruptive-innovation.

Clandinin, D. J., & Connelly, F. M. (1994). Personal experience methods. In N. K. Denzin & Y. S. Lincoln (Eds.), *Handbook of qualitative research* (pp. 413–427). Thousand Oaks: Sage Publications.

Murphy, M. S., Huber, J., & Clandinin, D. J. (2012). Narrative inquiry into two worlds of curriculum making. *LEARNing Landscapes, 5*(2), 219–235. https://doi.org/10.36510/learnland.v5i2.562

Doll, W. (1993). Changing paradigms. In W. Doll (Ed.), *A post-modern perspective on curriculum* (pp. 1–17). New York: Teachers College Press.

Edgerton, S. H. (2010). *Translating the curriculum: Multiculturalism into cultural studies.* Routledge. New York, NY

Feuerstein, M. Gonzalez, B. J., Porten, L., & Valens, K. (2014). Editor's preface. *The Barbara Johnson reader: The surprise of otherness.* (pp. xi–xvi). Durham: Duke University Press.

Frost, R. (2020/1915). *The Road Not Taken.* https://www.poetryfoundation.org/poems/44272/the-road-not-taken.

Home Box Office (HBO). (2020, Season1, Episode 7). *Silicon Valley.* https://www.hbo.com/silicon-valley.

Johnson, B. (2014). *The Barbara Johnson reader: The surprise of otherness.* In M. Feuerstein, B. J. Gonzalez, L. Porten, & K. Valens (Eds.). Durham: Duke University Press.

Kilgore, D. (2004). Toward a postmodern pedagogy. In R. St. Clair & J. Sandlin (Eds.), *Promoting critical practice in adult education* (pp. 46–53). San Francisco: Jossey-Bass.

Merriam-Webster. (2020). *Disrupt.* https://www.merriam-webster.com/dictionary/disrupt. (1995). Models of narrative analysis: A typology. *Journal of Narrative & Life History, 5*(2), 87–123.

Palmer, P. J. (2018). *On the brink of everything: Grace, gravity & getting old.* San Francisco: Berrett-Koehler.

Pinar, W. F. (2012). *What is curriculum theory?* (2nd ed.). New York: Routledge.

Pinar, W. F. (1994). *Autobiography, politics and sexuality: Essays in curriculum theory 1972–1992.* New York: Peter Lang.

Schlamb, C. (2017). On the practice of narrative landmarking: Navigating an ecological identity through self-study. In E. Lyle (Ed.), *At the intersection of selves and subject: Exploring the curricular landscape of identity* (pp. 41–52). Rotterdam: Sense Publishers.

Shields, C., & Reid-Patton, V. (2009). A curriculum of kindness: (Re) creating and nurturing heart and mind through teaching and learning. *Brock Education, 18*(2), 4–15.

Smith, T. (Mar 21, 2020). *Disruptive Technology*. Investopedia. https://www.investopedia.com/terms/d/disruptive-technology.asp.

Verizon Media. (2020). *Disrupt2020*. https://techcrunch.com/events/disrupt-sf-2020/.

5 Serendipity

Teresa Strong-Wilson

Serendipity describes a state of unexpected happiness brought on by accident or as if by accident. The term, first coined by Horace Walpole, described that happy condition of heroes who were continually "making discoveries, by accident and by sagacity, of things they were not in quest of" (Oxford English Dictionary, 1973, p. 2735). In the present piece, those individuals are readers who, by their own good fortune, come across the work of certain curriculum theorists whose writing (as well as persons) enrich their thinking – their sagacity – in serendipitous ways. In my own case, while several might be named, selected for this short piece are: William Pinar, Madeleine Grumet, Cynthia Chambers, Claudia Eppert, and Amarou Yoder. And while there might be many ways in which to show my gratitude to these curriculum scholars, the encomium, as a genre, offers scope for such expression. A version of the panegyric, the encomium praises the host (Hardison, Brogan, & Lewis, 2017). I am praising here the scholars whose presence and writing have hosted me, have invited me in, not once but many times over, through the generous capaciousness of their thought. In writing in this genre, I am inspired by W.G. Sebald's (2013) collection of essays, *A Place in the Country*, in which he expresses his wish to pay respect to those who have faithfully accompanied him in his travels, writers whose books or papers he chose to place in his suitcase or backpack – in short, those for whom he came to hold an "unwavering affection" (p. 1), and not only because of the subject they wrote about, but because of their manner of carrying themselves in the world.

My fuller entry into the writing and thinking of *William Pinar* was slow, marked by a delay of at least one decade and even, I would hazard, two. I encountered him first in person, in a seminar he taught, one among several rich offerings curated by Antoinette Oberg in the University of Victoria curriculum summer series of the nineties and early 2000's. I was a graduate student at the time. I was unaware of my good fortune in being there, at that time, among giants: William Pinar, Ted Aoki, William Doll, Cynthia Chambers (to name a few). I did not feel – and was never made to feel – them *as* giants; they were first and

DOI: 10.4324/9781003154112-6

Serendipity 53

foremost teachers who were also curriculum scholars, people who were deeply committed to curriculum as a "complicated conversation" (Pinar, 2009, p. 35), an interest that also infected me, by slow contagion. I recall that at the time I wanted, and needed, to find my own words, this after almost a decade of being away from academe, thoroughly immersed in being elementary teacher, wife and mother whose own sense of self had fallen dormant, as if in a state of suspension. I remember how tentative and vulnerable yet how *interested* I was as a graduate student and how, by his gracious presence, Bill (as much later I would feel comfortable calling him) was attuned to those feelings emanating from me, patiently encouraging me, with gentle force – demonstrating his interest in ideas shared and written – but without any pressure whatsoever to produce or go any other way than my own. Two small examples come to mind. "Teresa? It is good to see you here," Bill said, spying me, awkward and shy, as I held back from entering the salon of glittering talk at the Provoking Curriculum conference; his recognition gave me the courage to walk in and join the group. "I just write a short note saying that I am submitting this for your consideration," he said in response to my burning question about the then momentous-feeling task of presenting one's *self* to a journal editor in a submission email. I posed this question to him as we were seated at the Tim Horton's in the University of Victoria's Faculty of Education. What seemed complicated was rendered easy and without any sense of the situation being anything other than a discrete seeking for information, with advice discretely given. Here too was the pedagogical articulation and expression of *currere*, I realized several years later, his and Madeleine Grumet's reconceptualization of curriculum as grounded in the lived experience and biographic situation of the student, the one who studies (Pinar & Grumet, 2015).

Perhaps it was not so much that my own close reading of Bill's writing came late as that it grew in me, and with me, this as with the later 2000's, Bill also began to write about *currere* as social and subjective reconstruction. Several of his books stand thick with sticky notes on my "cardinal" book shelf. Thickest is *Towards a Poor Curriculum*, that seminal book that I only really "discovered," serendipitously, when, along with four other women curriculum scholars, we formed a reading group, becoming as "pilgrims" to the curriculum archive as we sought clarity, rejuvenation, and resolve (Strong-Wilson, Yoder, Aitken, Chang-Kredl & Radford, 2020). For my own part, I invariably found, and continue to find, in Bill's writing a language that helps me think; it is a language that, like Bill's presence, walks alongside me, allowing for that distinctiveness of self and other, that profound and radical respect that informs his writings as well as his way of carrying himself in the world.

I was sorry to have missed *Cynthia Chambers*' course; it was offered just as I had completed my doctoral coursework. I knew of Cynthia Chambers. In the grey filing cabinet in the Education Library could

54   Teresa Strong-Wilson

be found the well-thumbed manila folders of photocopied readings for Antoinette Oberg's Qualitative Inquiry course. It was here that I encountered the lucidity of Chambers' thinking; etymologically, its light: the pathways, and choices of pathways, which she evoked with such exacting humility and criticality as, walking in places that I could recognize, she sought out respectful ways of conducting research, both with the Indigenous peoples with whom she had grown up and was living – something that held immediate pertinence to my own research and biographic situation – but with human beings generally. Hers was a message of heart and head within a research landscape largely devoid of such quality of voice. Sorry to miss her course, she was kind enough to lend me a spiral bound copy of the course readings, which I did not return as promised, something I apologized for years later. It was that "unwavering affection" that kept me holding onto it (Sebald, 2013, p. 1), an affection that only grew with time and with opportunity to meet in person. I admired her integrity and disciplined mind even as I was drawn to her writing, especially the stories; how, with marvellous insight and craft, experience could be so precisely and incisively harnessed using words. Few could write – or speak; she was a very moving speaker – in ways at once vulnerable and unpretentious as well as intellectually penetrating. Her methods were rigorous. She seemed her harshest critic, sharing with her readers/listeners her moments of doubt, evasion, inattention, ones to which, if we could be as honest, we were all subject; so implicated, we followed her pathways through curricular terrain – by we, I mean myself as well as the many students with whom I shared her writing, including the contents of that spiral-bound binder. It was a pathway and process of re-membering the ground we were walking on; a place that if we could but listen and pay close attention, imparted meanings to be read and lived.

Madeleine Grumet has been among my greatest teachers even though I have never stepped in her classroom. I imagine my sense of excited anticipation, this accompanied by a feeling of sheer terror, at the prospect of *being* in her course, based on what I have read and re-read; based as well on the fleeting impressions I have had of her formidable, lively presence – this while standing opposite her around a dining room table at an American Association for the Advancement of Curriculum Studies (AAACS) party, or while occupying the same American Educational Research Association (AERA) conference elevator. I am not suggesting that Madeleine Grumet *is* terrifying; however, encountering her pedagogy at close-hand might be, for what it could elicit that I haven't yet imagined or foreseen but that she might – certainly would – perceive and ever so gently yet thoroughly intimate, this while wrapped in her green robe (Grumet, 2004). It would be the same green robe that as writer/ scholar, she wraps herself in for her own writing, that powerful, heady blend of theory and narrative/concrete example. When she tears herself

Serendipity 55

away and responds instead to student writing (a feeling I well know), it is in the same robe, with the same intensity of mind and emotion, that she applies herself to reading her student's autobiographical narratives. After receiving her feedback, I sense, one cannot be the same. It is not a writing/pedagogical practice that I consciously emulated; however, upon having encountered it, I recognized it as one that speaks to my own. And I wonder how I would feel being subjected to such tender, exacting insights; this at the crossroads where autobiography and intellectual integrity meet with such immediacy and force: an autobiographical curriculum field that, with Bill Pinar, Madeleine helped open.

Bill said that I should read and talk to *Claudia Eppert*. There was a delay, as is often my case. It can take (me) time to create spaces for what is important to do. Upon reading, Eppert's writings immediately marked me, startling me into thinking in ways I had not yet considered. It took several more years of all-too-brief meetings at CSSE and missed opportunities for those full-throated conversations to emerge. By mutual interest, she attended a talk I gave at McGill at a session of the Provoking Curriculum conference, as I attended hers. Then, as if by a colossal wave of unlooked for serendipity, Claudia was a visiting scholar at McGill from January to mid-March 2020, until COVID-19 intervened. During that interval, short as it was, time viscerally shifted with her co-presence: there over tea, there as I heard her speak at an event then reflected with her on the event, there in my graduate class as, after class, we travelled in the same metro car. I am aware that I am where she was before, in thinking through difficult conversations around *human* genocides within education. Her focus has shifted somewhat, however our talks reveal her abiding concern with sites of injustice and with our entangled implication as human beings. This concern continues to motivate her very deliberate finding of a pathway through difficult questions, but through a slow, inexorable movement, her utterly devastating thinking, with its power to disrupt, unravel and compel thinking anew.

I am grateful for *Amarou Yoder* and I am especially grateful for the experience of co-writing with Amarou. I suspect that I am not especially good at sharing writing space. However, with Amarou, I have been taught that this can be a highly enjoyable, and truly reciprocated, experience, this even as I recognize that, for our many affinities and likenesses, as writers and scholars we are quite, quite different. And I am profoundly grateful for being taught that difference because Amarou, who has been my doctoral student as well as co-teacher, friend and colleague, is someone for whom I have acquired the deepest respect. She has brought me to places where I cannot hope to travel in my own writing, but where, in that inimitable way of hers, Amarou can, as she beckons from her emerald field, inviting her reader to traverse this territory (not without its travails) with her. Reading Amarou's curriculum writing is to encounter serendipity itself, that happy congruence of a deeply embodied narrative

56 Teresa Strong-Wilson

voice evoking places she knows intimately or believes she knows, which wrestles with a more dispassionate, scholarly enquiring self. Both selves are ethically-motivated; however, ego and alter-ego vye for the page, ego sometimes dominating alter-ego, alter-ego sometimes chastening ego, with both bringing us somewhere we *want* to be: a place where we can live with our own ambiguity and limitations as well as a consciousness of gracious amplitude.

In one of Yeats' poems, a fifty-year old person (the poet himself, Yeats?) is sitting in a coffee-shop, alone, coffee cup emptied, book open. He looks up and gazes around, seeming to see the street but actually seeing, and feeling, much more. Yeats' poem continues: "My body all of a sudden blazed;/And twenty minutes more or less/It seemed, so great my happiness/That I was blessed and could bless" (Yeats, "Vacillation" IV; cited in Shelton, 2012, pp. 1–2 of 23). Was there a connection between the book being read and feeling that power of blessing and being blessed? Imagine ourselves there, at that coffee shop, or in a favourite chair at home. Like Sebald, we have with us cherished companions: writing by people and ideas we know or are coming to know better each time they are encountered. May we all have occasion to experience that serendipity – that "blazing" – that can course through us in encountering others' thoughts and presence: our vision enlarged, our lives invigorated. My own gratitude today is for those five curriculum scholars whose paths, happily, have crossed my own.

References

Grumet, M. (2004). My green robe: Scholae personae. In S. Weber and C. Mitchell (Eds.), *Not just any dress: Narratives of memory, body and identity* (pp. 89–98). Peter Lang.

Hardison, O. B., Brogan, T. V. F. & Lewis, F. (2017). Panegyric. In R. Greene & S. Cushman (Eds.), *The Princeton Encyclopedia of poetry and poetics* (4th ed.) [online version]. Princeton University Press.

Oxford English Dictionary. (1973). *The compact edition of the Oxford English Dictionary.* Oxford University Press.

Pinar, W. (2009). *The worldliness of cosmopolitan education: Passionate lives in public service.* Routledge.

Pinar, W. & Grumet, M. (2015). *Toward a poor curriculum.* Educator's International Press.

Sebald, W. (2013). *A place in the country.* Hamish Hamilton.

Shelton, C.A. (2012). Gratitude: Considerations from a moral perspective. In R.A. Emmons and M.E. McCullough (Eds.), *The psychology of gratitude.* Oxford Scholarship Online. DOI:10.1093/acprof:oso/9780195150100.003.0013

Strong-Wilson, T., Yoder, A., Aitken, A., Chang-Kredl, S. & Radford, L. (2020). Currere tales: Journeying as pilgrims to the (an)archive. In T. Strong-Wilson, C. Ehret, D. Lewkowich & S. Chang-Kredl (Eds.), *Provoking curriculum encounters across educational experience: New engagements with the curriculum theory archive* (pp. 8–20). Routledge.

6 The Labyrinth of Gratitude
A Collage of Memories, Reflections and Gifts in Learning and Teaching

Marni J. Binder

> I enter
> I take that first step
> trepidatious
> like dipping my toe into
> the ocean to test mood, temperature
> The dynamic rhythms of changing tides.

Looking back on a lengthy teaching career spanning many decades in public education and now academia, I am reminded of the many gifts received from mentors who guided me and the children and families who inspired me. Parker J. Palmer (1998) reminds us that it is our mentors who "awaken a truth within us, a truth we can reclaim years later by recalling their impact on our lives" (p. 72).

In this chapter, I explore these gifts and memories through the metaphor of the labyrinth. The labyrinth offers short and long paths that lead to and away from the center: the heart of one's being and the opportunity to examine deeply the landscapes of meaningful experiences that influence our lives. The labyrinth is a mirror for the inner self (West, 2011) and a place to explore the sacred in our lives, the mysterious pulls and influences that present themselves throughout one's lived experiences. Bickel and Jordan (2009) discuss the labyrinth as "a unifying symbol to learn/teach and inquire within and from" (p. 2).

In the spring of 2014, I walked the labyrinth in High Park in Toronto, Canada. This walking ritual, and the symbolic nature of the labyrinth remained in my thoughts, and since then I have walked several more. And so, with the labyrinth as my metaphor, I move back and forth in time. Memories become timeless, visceral, sensual, and relational and it is in these liminal spaces that curriculum theory and my practice converge.

DOI: 10.4324/9781003154112-7

58 *Marni J. Binder*

Image 6.1 Photocollage of Labyrinths, by Marni Binder, April 2015

I have received many gifts in my personal and professional life and am grateful to have been embraced by such loving scholarly souls comprised of children, families and learning communities. A collage of image, poetic responses and text, and interludes of inspiration, bring these memories to life, embodying a future of hope in my storied future. The reader is invited to walk this labyrinth journey with me as I remember the gift of mentorship, embrace with gratitude the gift of friendship and received the gift of teaching. These gifts are not isolated and often interweave, overlap in, through and with the storied experiences shared.

And so I journeyed… and so I shifted…

And so I stepped in, out… breath… the (re)emerging Journey

The Labyrinth of Gratitude

Image 6.2 Photograph of Marni Binder in the Labyrinth, McClelland Sculpture Park and Gallery, Langwarrin Melbourne Australia taken by Jane Bone October 11, 2014

The Gift of Mentorship: David Booth

interlude:
    as I enter
    i ask
what would David say?
    as I return…

I first met David Booth (1939–2019) in 1993 towards the end of my Master of Education studies at OISE/UT in an "Arts in Education" course. I can recall wondering who this humorous and thought provoking professor was. He challenged us to rethink the meaning of the arts in the lives of children/students we taught and the importance of not

60 Marni J. Binder

just being consumers of curriculum. David spoke with conviction about the importance of meaning-making, storied lived experiences and community. He exemplified what Ted Aoki (1993b, 2005) spoke of when he described the "language of the lived curriculum" where "life is embodied in the very stories and language people speak and live" (p. 207).

I can hear the passion in his voice as he spoke of the many students he had worked with over the years, the agency of voice created through the arts. I remember thinking "I would like to see him do this with the Senior Kindergarten/1/2 classroom I teach in Regent Park." And so, I asked. And so, he came and wove his story drama magic.

Image 6.3 Photograph of David Booth Taken by Jay Booth, 2011

> eyes wide open
> mesmerized
> enchanted
> captivated
> deep listening
>
> my ed assistant and I raised our hands
> when he asked a question.

And so, began our journey together: mentor, colleagues and friends. David's uncanny understanding of one's potential would plant seeds to

The Labyrinth of Gratitude 61

nudge you forward in a good way. Though a story shared before, this was *the* significant moment in my career path, where one afternoon, shortly after completing my Master of Education, we were discussing my career plans, possible next steps. David said, "I think you should continue." When I realized he was referring to beginning doctoral studies, I said "why?." His response, "Because you have something to contribute" (Binder, 2012, p. 118).

words holding a special place
   never forgotten
(re)shaping
   transforming
supporting
   guiding
through challenges
provoking thought
i pay it forward
through in with
lived time
   with others
you taught me to
   tap dance
backwards
   pause
to move forward
   (re)discover
the voice of curriculum
i dream of you
and you guide me

David taught me to dwell in the curriculum creatively, to move in, through and with, to engage in what William Pinar (2011) referred to as "a complicated conversation" (p. 73). These multi-layered discourses of complexities become what Rebecca Lloyd (2018) spoke of as "curriculum- as- living- experience" (p. 26).

Our storied lives continued to intersect on so many occasions. From my doctoral journey, to the richness of classroom teaching and leadership roles, David just knew where I would land. I still see his proud smile as he stepped into my new office at Ryerson University. Our lunches would be filled with animated talk as we caught up on new learnings, travels; intimate sharing between colleagues and friends.

I recall how we finally set a date to meet, it had been awhile and overdue. Life has an elusive way of changing the course of events in one's life and is often too sudden.

62   *Marni J. Binder*

Friday December 21, 2019
1:00 tic toc
1:15 tic toc
1:30 tic toc
1:45 tic toc

how long had it been?

emailed Monday
excited to see each other
too long
missed
often
asking
what would David say?

so much
to ask
wisdom needed
navigating confusing
directions blurred

TIC TOC
called your home
office dark
returned to the pub
sat alone at the Duke

2:00
left
not being able to
accept
the fear
in my heart

December 23
a post on FB
you were gone

as I waited
you began   to leave
transition
a date missed
a missed date
tears of sadness
memories past present

smile at my future

The Gift of Friendship

interlude:
  as I step in
  I remember
kind conversations
  as I return...

I was first introduced to Bob Steele's (1925–2018) work by David Booth when I was just starting my doctoral work at the OISE/UT. I can still hear his voice: "here, you can borrow this book. Your thesis is here. You can't keep it. You must buy it yourself." The book was, *Draw Me a Story*, published in 1998. And so, I bought it and kept it close. Bob Steele was 75 when he published this first book. At the time I was a classroom teacher of grade one/two children in what was then called the "inner city" in Toronto. I could relate to his ideas about children in my daily teaching practice, particularly the importance of drawing as language, the authenticity of children's artwork and what he defined as *aesthetic energy*, "the flow of emotional response" through the experience felt when they draw (Binder, 2017, p. 9).

In July of 2004, I was going to Vancouver to present my thesis work at The Imagination and Education Conference at Simon Fraser University. I decided to email Bob and ask if I could meet him. I spent a delightful afternoon with him and his wife Mary over tea and cookies. And so, began a wonderful friendship through email correspondence, phone conversations and visits when I was in Vancouver. I received his newsletters from the Drawnet website he created for teachers and parents and was a grateful recipient of his gifted self-published books and lengthy emails musing about the state of art education locally and nationally and the critical necessity of the arts in the lives of children. Bob's presence was always there in my teaching. When I left the classroom to teach at the university level, he remained with me and still does. I keep his books close. I keep his memory close.

His work pushed my thinking about children's drawing and representation as intentional, communicative and in many cases conversational. The children I taught reinforced numerous times what Bob was trying to bring to the world of education. I can recall having a discussion with the children in this particular grade one/two class. I asked, "Why is art important?" There were many responses, but one stood out: "You draw first to think what you write." The children drew and wrote stories daily. The time spent on drawing far exceeded the time with text initially and even when both complemented each other, drawing was the prime mode to communicate, express and reflect their understanding of the world. The children would delightfully chat with each other as they played in, with and through their drawings. Bob's discourse of "drawing

64 Marni J. Binder

Image 6.4 Photograph of Lino Block and Print of Bob Steele Taken by Artist Peter Scurr, June 25, 2020

Image 6.5 Photograph of Lino Block and Print of Bob Steele Taken by Artist Peter Scurr, June 25, 2020

The Labyrinth of Gratitude   65

as a language in its own right" (Steele, 1998, p. 9) and the importance of a daily draw came alive in the classroom. The children would share their unique signatures and identities through the drawings they created.

After 23 years of teaching in the public school system, career directions changed as I entered academia. For a number of years, I have taught a literacy course to third year students and a creative arts/visual arts course to second year students. In both of these courses, I draw on the work of Bob Steele. Bob's ideas on aesthetic energy continued to inform, extend, and engage the students I teach. I play and encourage my students to play. Nachmanovitch (1990), stated: "play is the taproot from which original art springs" (p. 42). It is this taproot that is Bob Steele's aesthetic energy.

Bob was drawing and writing daily right up to his death at the age of 93. We had been emailing a week before, checking in on each other and chatting about education and the arts. He never stopped challenging the status quo in politics and education and continued to have several projects on the go. I remember him as a passionate educator, artist, and author. I remember him as my friend.

Gift of Teaching

> interlude:
>   as i step in
>   i see
> smiling faces
>   as i return...

It has always been a privilege to experience the awe and wonder children have shared with me over the many years I taught in schools in the downtown of Toronto. Ayers (2010) spoke about how teaching "is never far from mystery" (p. 135). Their ways of seeing and being in the world, the expression of their inner lives through the everyday has been a constant source of joy. These experiences have shaped my conceptual explorations, enlightened my personal creative endeavours and informed my work as a holistic and artistic educator and researcher. I bring to my teaching now a collective learning and understanding that has evolved from the experiences during those years. I have never left the world of these children and the community.

The community I spent 23 years, Regent Park, in was one of the most diverse in my city. The parents and the children were my first teachers. Different cultures, languages and religions converged harmoniously in the learning space. I cherish the memories of parents coming on field trips with me, and the excitement for learning they had. I also developed relationships that were built on trust and care. This gave me permission to create an arts-based learning space.

66 *Marni J. Binder*

    embody learning
        the cosmology of childhood
   to live
     aesthetically
     spiritually
     in the world
        present to the voices
     hearts minds spirits
   of children
          Binder, 2020

Image 6.6 Photograph of Artwork by Grade 2 student, 2004, Taken by Marni Binder, July 2020

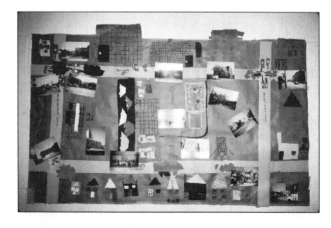

Image 6.7 Photograph of Artwork by Grade 1/2 students, 2001: *The School Block*. Photograph by Marni Binder

The children's unique signature is what built the learning community. Their agentic presence and voices created the learning space; the living curriculum. Partnerships with parents and extended community was part of this. Their "being" was the pedagogical experience I bring to my teaching today and how to create a classroom community based on reciprocity of being and sharing. I hold the collective spirit of the children and the community I taught in with gratitude and bring them into my own mindful creative spaces, where I am reminded to hold onto my awe, wonder, the sensual and the everyday.

end/lude

We are living in unforeseen times and I am writing in extraordinary conditions in a global pandemic where introspection, meaning and lived experience retreat into the memories of the past and dwell there with gratitude. Antress (2006) reminds me that "the walk out of the labyrinth is realistically and symbolically the act of taking what we have received out into the world. This is an empowering and integrating part of the walk" (p.78). It is a gift to be able to walk with and honour those whose profound influence and presence in my life was transformative in shaping my scholarship, teaching and artistic practice. I view this recursive learning as one that continues to travel with me as I reflect on and curate my teaching and academic work and how this also informed my former leadership role as the Learning and Teaching Chair for my faculty at Ryerson.

And so, I end as I begin, re/storying, re/journeying and once again I find myself feeling

that first step
    trepidatious
    like dipping my toe into
    the ocean to test mood, temperature
The dynamic rhythms of changing tides.

And I (re)emerge) and enter.

References

Antress, L. (2006). *Rediscovering the labyrinth as a spiritual practice*. New York, NY: Riverhead Books.

Aoki, T. (1993b, 2005). Legitimizing lived curriculum: Toward a curricular landscape of multiplicity. In. W.F. Pinar & R.L. Irwin (Eds.), *Curriculum in a new key: The collected works of Ted Aoki*. (pp. 199–215). Mahwah, NJ: Lawrence Erlbaum.

Ayers, W. (2010). *To teach: The journey of a teacher* (3rd ed.). New York, NY: Teachers College Press.

68 Marni J. Binder

Bickel, B., & Jordon, N. A. (2009). Labyrinths as ritual art: A pedagogy of inquiry/witnessing/listening to the sacred. *Educational Insights, 13*(2), 1–6. Retrieved from http://www.barbarabickel.ca/resources/LabyrinthAsRitualArt_EI_bickel_jordan.pdf.

Binder, M. J. (2012). Teaching as lived research. *Childhood Education, 88*(2), 118–120.

Binder, M. J. (2017). In *conversation with Bob Steele. In* M. J. Binder & S. Kind (Eds.). *Drawing as language: Celebrating the work of Bob Steele,* (pp. 1–12). Rotterdam, The Netherlands: Sense Publishers.

Lloyd, R. (2018). Invocation-curriculum- as living- experience. In E. Hasebe-Ludt & C. Leggo (Eds.), *Canadian curriculum studies,* (p. 26). Toronto, ON: Canadian Scholars.

Palmer, P. J. (2017). *The courage to teach* (20th anniversary ed.). San Francisco, CA: Jossey-Bass.

Pinar, W. F. (2011). *What is curriculum theory?* New York, NY: Routledge.

Steele, B. (1998). *Draw me a story.* Winnipeg, MB: Peguis Publishers.

West, M. G. (2011). *Exploring the labyrinth: A guide for healing and Spiritual growth.* New York, NY: Crown Publishing.

7 Opening to Grace

Curricular Knowing as Spiritual Praxis

Sarah MacKenzie-Dawson

Grace exists in the questions. Opening to grace allows us to live and listen within the questions, as we become connected to a knowing that expands far beyond our own consciousness or experience. This chapter is about opening to grace as a way to know self and world, to connect with something greater than ourselves. It is here, as we situate ourselves within the questions, that curriculum becomes a spiritual practice of presence and transformation. Curriculum theory, Pinar (2004) suggests, asks one to reflect upon one's "position as engaged," actively involved "in the construction of a public sphere, a public sphere not yet born, a future that cannot be discerned in, or even thought from, the present. So conceived, the classroom becomes simultaneously a civic square and a room of one's own" (pp. 36–37). The classroom is not bound by walls, but rather exists as a fluid place of experience where we might not cling to the known, but rather open ourselves to the unknown – open ourselves to grace. Opening to grace, the first principle of *Anusara* yoga, is a practice of body and mind where we are directed to first set the foundation, connecting ourselves to the earth, becoming vulnerable and engaged. It is a practice of opening ourselves to the flow and rhythm of our be(com)ing, in connection to the world, to one another, and ourselves.

When I began to work on this chapter, I had a plan, and then in a moment my relationship to knowing, my relationship to the world changed. I was reminded of impermanence and the ever-evolving nature of experience. The only means to endure was to open myself to grace – to become present within the experience. Curriculum lives in the stories of experience, in the overlapping moments of inter-action with life and one another. We seek knowledge, connection, truth, and within education this is often reflected in memorization and performance within expectation and definition. However, Tippet (2017) intimates that "[p]rofound truth, like the vocabulary of virtue, eludes formulation ... [b]ut put a spiritual insight to a story, an experience, a face; describe where it anchors in the ground of your being; and it will change you in the telling and others in the

DOI: 10.4324/9781003154112-8

70 Sarah MacKenzie-Dawson

listening" (p. 22). Poetic inquiry allows me to enter deeply into the (un)known, into relationship, into a space of curricular knowing as spiritual practice – spiritual praxis. It creates space for listening, for dialogue, disruption, interpretation, connection, and possibility, as I consciously and actively open myself up to a current that is bigger than my knowing, a current that connects us all. Across the landscape of this chapter, I draw upon poetic inquiry as a way to enter the story, to thoughtfully meander through experience as I engage in the practice of opening to grace. Through the poetic and personal, I seek to consider experience as an opening – an opportunity to listen, to gain insight, a space of curricular be(com)ing. Within poetry, my stories exist as questions, places of pause and being, gentle grooves along the curricular landscape of (un)knowing within experience. And so, I step into messiness, into the questions, the space, into the (un)known, and into experience.

3.48 Million confirmed cases
today
61, 834 new cases
today
138, 000 deaths, 787 new
today
3 weeks
    they say
we will all know loss,
the breath of tomorrow
trapped in a web
of questions
yearning
    for the (un)namable

Our knowing is shaped by moments, it is temporal, fluid, fleeting. If I had begun this chapter a year ago my mind would be very much focused on other things. I would have been feeling ambivalent about my oldest daughter starting kindergarten. I would have been feeling overwhelmed as I anticipated the start of another semester and trying hard to savour those last few days of vacation time. I may have had a moment of "what if" cross my mind, but it would have been simply a moment and then I would move forward in my assumption of the familiar – what I knew as normalcy. When the pandemic came everything changed. I was blessed (and burdened) with an excessive amount of time with my immediate family and overwhelmed by having to balance the various facets of my personal and professional lives. Months have passed and I look at the numbers, finding myself facing decisions that might, perhaps, mean life or death: whether to send my children back to school; whether to attend

Opening to Grace 71

my yoga teacher training in person; which family members to interact with, knowing that some think the pandemic is nothing more than a farce and have gone on with their lives. The world has changed, it is always changing. I have changed, I am always changing. I feel like I am navigating without roots as I search in the dark for some sense of peace or awareness of the right thing to do.

Stillness weeps
    political wretchedness
does not whisper,
it screams
whipping humanity
wiping away
the few cinders of connection
that remain
I am with/out
listening
    to preaching without the pastoral
May love fill this empty space where
beings become violent
powered by the idolatry of answers
that echo with/in the ideal
that satisfies
    craving
for a moment
What happens
when the pink clouds of satisfaction dissipate,
when the answers crumble?

> "The pursuit of an ideal excludes love, and without love no human problem can be solved."
>
> (Krishnamurti, 1953, p. 27)

I find it apropos that I am writing this chapter during a pandemic, a time when everything that we have been attached to becomes disrupted: our learning, our work, our relationships. In this moment, I have no answers; to move forward I must open myself to grace – to love, as I engage with the messiness that is life. Dewey (1980) so thoughtfully reminds:

> [L]ife is no uniform uninterrupted march or flow. It is a thing of histories, each with its own plot, its own inception and movement towards its close, each having its own particular rhythmic movement; each with its own unrepeated quality pervading it throughout (pp. 35–36)

72 Sarah MacKenzie-Dawson

Throughout
   with/in
my breath washes over me
a collaboration
of time and space
Light whispers
gather across my consciousness
with/out and with/in
a body, mind, spirit
amidst
the violent rustling of leaves
that scratch my gentle thoughts
where sadness and grief gather
like puddles
Peace ripples in space
flooding the waters of my being
breath
   and light and love
my hand to my heart
my heart to my hand
I am breath
I am love
I am light
   open and connected
flowing in the rhythmic motions
of time and being

To engage with these rhythms, I must breathe (re)turning myself to the moment. It is a practice that allows us to attend to experience, to embrace Pinar's (2004) suggestion to "listen to one's silence, observe the shadows among which one moves" (p. 126).

Caught up in the circling
   cacophony of being human
body and heart and mind,
spirit writhing in a storied web
We gather together
   feet planted
gravity and ground our foundation
Body and heart and mind and spirit
held by breath
and the (im)perfect nature
of being
human

Opening to Grace 73

Curriculum is about navigating in the dark, finding our ways amidst, and it is about relationship with something greater than self. It is about listening and opening ourselves up to grace and possibility, about learning to breathe and becoming present. I did not always think about curriculum this way; there was a time when I found myself absorbed by a yearning for answers. If one were to ask me, at the beginning of my career, why I chose to go into the field of education, what would immediately come to mind is all that was wrong in my own experience as a learner; not being seen, being silenced, feeling forced to conform. We are all drawn to education for some reason or another, for me it was about being lost, about not being seen as a learner. I spent a lot of time thinking about what was wrong with education. I was closed off, judgmental and yearning for something I could not name. It has taken me a long time to get to where I am, but today when someone asks me, "Why education?" I can honestly say it is about listening, about being connected to something larger than myself and creating the space for others to become present within the chaotic, painful and blissful experience of life. Ask me today where education resides and I will tell you everywhere. When I spent my time focused on fixing, I discounted the uniqueness of experience and person. I imposed myself – my values, my experience, my desires and expectations upon the experience, rather than taking the time to listen. Irigaray (1999) offers the insight that "our culture, our school education, our cultural formation want it this way: to learn, to know, is to make one's own through instruments of knowledge capable, we believe, of seizing, of taking, of dominating all of reality, all that exists, all that we perceive, and beyond" (p. 121). When we begin to let go of that sense of domination, when we begin to open ourselves up to grace, we do not find the answers or fix what we identify as wrong with education, but instead learn to live as Rilke (1986) suggests, within the questions (p. 34). We learn to connect to ourselves as multi-dimensional beings, body/mind/spirit, as people who love, who struggle, who stumble. I stumble, but by embracing the mind of the beginner, opening myself, and aligning myself with something greater than myself, I might learn outside expectation and within spiritual space. This is what Miller (2000) refers to when talking about the "soulful curriculum," that which "gives priority to the inner life...seeks a balance and connection between our inner and outer lives (p. 49)

There is stillness
in the morning
where light and dark
intermingle in whispers
where the monologue of shame
dances with breath of peace,

74 *Sarah MacKenzie-Dawson*

space, opening
    body, heart, mind
My heart is tight
    caught in the stories of
my own
failure,
    what
I did/did not do
        echoing
        burden,
needs wrapped up in the complex
packaging of our human nature.
In the morning
    the aching of my heart
rustles the stillness
    opening my consciousness
to what
I could not hear before
        the heart of the child
caught in the wound of my own
forgetting.
      Moments of awakeness/awareness,
stillness stirred by gravity,
I am planted,
participating
in this delicate dance,
      where life is not bound
        by the apertures of expectation,
but by listening,
by love (un)fastened

We learn within the unexpected openings. I try to write in the morning,
but these days I am often distracted by the ongoing presence of my two
daughters, distracted by their needs – their own practices of being. This
is not how I imagined my working process. I hate to admit, but I resent
that all my plans for writing have been so deeply disrupted by a pandemic
that has changed so much of what daily life looks like. While I can never
truly separate my working life from my family life, my personal life, the
reality of this is magnified in this moment. I have to remember the wise
words of Leggo (2008): "There is no need to separate the personal from
the professional any more than we can separate the dancer from the
dance. The personal and professional always work together, in tandem,
in union, in the way of complementary angles" (p. 5). His words remind
me to open myself to grace, to be present to what is happening in this
moment, to learn from and in the experience: personal and professional.

Opening to Grace 75

Prediction is predicated
with/in closure,
postures of (dis)awareness
disrupted by requirements of want
waiting, boundaries
that close
space,
       space
breath
life
   the body bears

"Oppositions of mind and body, soul and matter, spirit and flesh
all have their origin, fundamentally, in fear of what life might bring
forth"
(Dewey, 1980, p. 22).

Paralyzed by the murkiness of being
     powerless
   He started coughing yesterday
   the man I love, the father of my children,
   my partner, who now rests quietly upstairs,
 too tired
   all I have for him is a handful of vitamins
as we wade through our human fragility

I do not know what will happen in the future and this scares me. All I
can do in this moment is breathe and be present, opening myself to what
might be revealed – even within the unwanted or unexpected. How often
our purpose and intention within the field of education is conflicted with
the quest for answers and transcendence, movement toward something
we rarely cannot name. There is irony within this quest as it leads us
fixed within a closed space of expectation and attachment, where the
body/mind/spirit/heart is bound by the intangible answer. When we
open to grace, we become a part of something larger than self, larger
than the answers, we become part of a current that allows the mind/
body/spirit/heart to awaken to experience, to be present, entering into
connection with self and other, past, present, and future.

Where breath
  and light
  echo within
     the substantial space
     of body, being
  soft and subtle strength

76 *Sarah MacKenzie-Dawson*

a (re)turning to
the center
a (re)turning to
heart
to the dance
of body, spirit, mind
a (re)turning to
the simplicity of breath
delightfully, (im)perfectly
connected

Curricular knowing does not exist within a vacuum, it is shaped by our experiences, our encounters. Each encounter is an opportunity to open ourselves to grace, to learn to live within the questions and it is here where our knowing becomes a work of spiritual praxis.

References

Dewey, J. (1980). *Art as experience*. New York, NY: Perigree Books.

Irigaray, L. (1999). *Between east and west: From singularity to community*. New York, NY: Columbia University Press.

Krishnamurti, J. (1953). *Education and the significance of life*. New York, NY: HarperCollins.

Leggo, C. (2008). Autobiography: Researching our lives and living our research. In S. Springgay, R. L. Irwin, C. Leggo & P. Gouzouasis (Eds.), *Being with a/r/tography* (pp. 3–23). Rotterdam: Sense Publishers.

Miller, J. (2000). *Education and the soul: Toward a spiritual curriculum*. Albany: SUNY Press.

Pinar, B. (2004). *What is curriculum theory*. Mahwah, NJ: Lawrence Erlbaum Associates, Publishers.

Rilke, R.M. (1986). *Letters to a young poet*. New York, NY: Vintage Books.

Tippet, K. (2017). *Becoming wise: An inquiry into the mystery and art of living*. New York, NY: Penguin Books.

8 Pedagogical Resonances
A Curriculum of Care

Walter Gershon

Our lives as academics are as deeply influenced by possibilities from those we may never meet as those with whom we see daily. Conceptualizing how we come to be, always a false suspension of ever-unfolding understandings, is a never-ending entanglement of things. These entanglements are affecting and effecting reverberations and resonances that echo in anticipated and unexpected ways. Rather than untangle such threads, this chapter presents a particular entanglement of my scholarly self. Boni Wozolek (2021) speaks of this work as a forms of pathology, tracing patterns after they have emerged so that one can learn from their movements and add them to one's conceptualizations of what might yet come to be.

I am an inefficient thinker. My feelings and thoughts flit about, lead me down rabbit holes I follow all the way to the end, skip across literatures and generations, connect clearly oppositional positions, borrow with veracity, well up out of seemingly nowhere and often recede as quickly as they arrived. Over time, I have both come to accept and count on these intuitions. They are, as is likely no surprise to anyone who knows me, improvisational. What varies is not their improvisational nature but the kind of improvising involved, from personal interpretations of longstanding themes to those that eschew structures except for the ones that emerge in the making.

That I don't believe in a solitary, retroactively assembled line of inquiry as a sign of an academic life well lived is also probably not surprising. Instead, I understand the organizing principles for what it is I may be doing as a curriculum scholar more akin to an atlas, an ordering of the world that is the result of sustained consideration of never-ending interrelated wanderings, expressing different understandings that somehow form a collective whole. That such a collective whole is always already incomplete is also central to how I conceptualize my life as a curriculum scholar and the construction of this chapter. This chapter, then, is an incomplete tracing of one way I might order the task this fine group of editors has provided.

DOI: 10.4324/9781003154112-9

78   *Walter Gershon*

A Polyphonic Pathology

Sounds have governed my life and I have always been someone who is attuned to the sensory, as sensitivities and aesthetics for example, for better and worse. They are central and foregrounded in who I am regardless of how they manifest or the fit of such manifestations to understandings and sociocultural contexts. As much of how I have approached the sonic is through musical forms of its organizations, I begin here with a stream of teachers who have made my musical life what it is today:

> Martha Weiss my first piano teacher (at three) and friend/care-taker throughout my childhood; Frank Ball, middle school band teacher who started a jazz band in 1982–83, very early goings for such programs; Jeffrey Davidson, my high school choir teacher who not only provided helped me understand how to think about sounds and singing but also created safe spaces for noncompliant students for whom even a great public high school was a tough fit; Harold Ashenfelter who helped push me towards theory and whose copy of *158 Saxophone Exercises* (Rascher, 1968) often sits on my music stand; Maura Bank, my first percussion teacher and sister from another mother; Angel Luis Figueroa who schooled my hands, ushering me into the Los Angeles percussion community including teachers Maestros Lazaro Galarraga and Jesus Alfonso Miro, Munyungo Jackson, and Luca Brandoni; Badal Roy and John B. Williams who helped me better understand how to be myself as a musician not to mention introductions to a ton of amazing cats; VR Venkatarman who was walking me through the world of South Indian percussion before I left LA for the midlands; and Reagan Mitchell who continues to think with me about all things musical, helping to fill in the gaps.

The persistence might be in part nature but it is these wonderful people who helped me refine my own understandings of practice and sonic expression in musical forms.

Steven Feld's (1982) *Sound and Sentiment: Birds Weeping, Poetics, and Song in Kaluli Expression* and Richard and Sally Price's (Price & Price, 1991) *Two Evenings in Saramaka*, deeply impacted my understanding of what books might do. *Two Evenings in Saramaka* was a revelation: two full days of music and ritual transcribed in words and musical notation. It has been a while since I've read the work through and would undoubtedly find certain kinds of essentialism and conflation between event, ritual, and culture, realizing that "a book" could have this kind of use and architecture just amazed me. It was not only Feld's book and associated work, nor only his construct of acoustemology that

Pedagogical Resonances 79

still resides in my understandings, but also that Feld released an album of field recordings. Books with sounds, in sound, through sounds.

Steven Feld has also been influential in at least three additional ways to my life as a scholar: his co-edited book with Keith Basso (Feld & Basso, 1996) was foundational in thinking about how sounds and critical geography (thank you Rob Helfenbein and Jan Nespor) might combine; Feld's interview with Donald Brenneis (2004) "Doing Anthropology in Sound," (Feld & Brenneis, 2004) provided leverage for what I call sonic ethnography; and Feld was personally encouraging when I reached out to him as I did my due diligence developing that methodology.

Just as I would likely have given up exploring questions of sound in education were it not for a particularly well-timed email conversation with Maxine Greene (Gershon, 2017), I would not have this career without Deborah Wong whose methods in ethnomusicology course I took as an additional methods course during my doctoral studies. Dr. Wong is an ethnomusicologist extraordinaire whose scholarship at the intersection of gender, race, and ethnomusicology is as foundational as it is ongoing. From the outset of the course, I rubbed her the wrong way. This, for the record, is on me, a combination of being a doctoral student who had learned some of the ideas presented in a methods class for Masters students and my own ongoing experiences studying and playing in Los Angeles. Mea culpa Dr. Wong. Among the things learned in her course was the possibility of approaching recording research ecologies with the same techniques one might use to record live music and to the work of Paul Stoller whose *Taste of Ethnographic Things: The Senses in Anthropology* (Stoller, 1989) and *Sensuous Scholarship* (Stoller, 1997) became foundational in my understandings of methodology and education.

In education, Liora Bresler has been a touchstone for me as she has for so many over her stellar career. I first met Liora through her writing, particularly her pieces in *Arts Education Policy Review* (e.g., Bresler, 1995, 1998). Then, through a combination of events, I chaired a session that Liora organized including Alma Gottleib and Philip Graham and at which I first met my scholarly twin Kim Powell whose work I had been introduced to in George Spindler's last edited collection (Powell, 2006). It was Liora Bresler who first introduced me to Oded ben Horin through whom I first visited Norway and, on a leg of my return flight from Amsterdam to Chicago, met Biljana Fredriksen who was, but of course, on her way to do a Fulbright with Liora and who would be my connection to the University of Southeast Norway during my sabbatical in 2017.

While I have had an opportunity to share this with both scholars, it is worth reiterating how my career remains indebted to Paul Stoller and David Howes. Paul was quite generous when we met and his work continues to be a force in my scholarship. David has been supportive

80 Walter Gershon

and available since I first reached out to him as a newly minted Ph.D. and his work in the field of sensory studies, not least of which are his own scholarship (e.g., Howes, 2003), the collections he has edited (e.g., Howes, 1991, 2005) and co-edited, and the readers in his series for Berg Press. For example, Michael Bull and Les Back's (Bull & Back, 2004) *The Auditory Culture Reader* in that series – along with work from scholars such as Jonathan Sterne (2003), Veit Erlmann (2004), and Jim Drobnick (2004) – helped me better understand that the works I'd been reading separately across fields and disciplines had truly coalesced into something called sound or sonic studies.

Returning to education and the sonic, it is impossible to overestimate how influential Fredrick Erickson, Greg Dimitradis, and Ted T. Aoki's work has been on my career. I met Fred a few times before his retirement, first at a three-hour workshop on ethnography at University of California, Los Angeles that Reba arranged for those doing interpretive scholarship during my doctoral studies and a few times after at various conferences. That he remembered me at all is due to a citation while work was in progress and my first publication on classroom interactions as collective improvising. (As but another note of these entanglements, this article won an award from the Narrative and Research SIG of the American Educational Research Association. It was at this ceremony I first met two other award winners, Jeong-Hee Kim and Jerry Rosiek, along with Jean Clandinen who presented these awards as chair). For the first decade of my time doing academic work, from the start of my doctoral studies through my first years as an assistant professor, it seemed as though everything I thought I'd "found" in my own research were ideas, possibilities, and challenges that Erickson had published, often 15 or 20 years before I'd considered them.

Greg Dimitriadis was an intellectual force and a really wonderful person. Greg, the first person in curriculum studies, very early in my career, to truly hear my thoughts about classrooms, sound, and improvising and a person whose scholarship continually helped me think through a variety of ideas and connections, scholarly, and otherwise. I was also one of the many people Greg supported over the years formally and informally, from showing up to sessions, and eventually my students' sessions, to writing formal letters of support.

I never had the pleasure of meeting Ted T. Aoki. Introduced to his work in passing during my dissertation, it was Bill Pinar and Rita Irwin's (Pinar and Irwin, 2005) compilation of Aoki's scholarship that did the trick. The primacy of the eye, the introduction of jazz improvising as tools for teaching future teachers, connections to aesthetics and Japanese philosophies (my B.A. was in East Asian Studies), a thoughtful, tone that embedded critiques in dignity, it was all there. In Aoki, I found both ideas I hadn't considered and words for ideas I had yet to learn.

Bill Pinar has been and continues to be a friend and mentor since we first met during my second year of doctoral studies at my first ever conference, the 2001 Curriculum and Pedagogy Conference at the University of Victoria. I was never officially a student of Bill's at any institution. Instead, I was one of many doctoral students Bill found and decided to think with over time, an important lesson from Greg and George Noblit as well. In this context, in addition to many other moments, the reason *Sound Curriculum: Sonic Studies in Educational Theory, Method, and Practice* exists is because Bill suggested it. In that slightly casual delivery that notes the seriousness of the suggestions without the pressure to fulfil its promise he said something like, maybe you should think about putting all those sound ideas together in a book; you could pitch it to my series. I had honestly not considered that option before the suggestion.

As with Bill Pinar, I never studied under George Noblit though a good number of my friends and colleagues did. George is another person who became a friend and mentor in ways that blossomed over time. Another musician/scholar, George has helped me think through many ideas about relationships between education and the arts, the relationship between aesthetics, methodology, and justice, and many other such possibilities. Ming Fang He and Bill Schubert have not only championed my career but also my scholarship. As but one pair of examples, I served on the programme committee for Division B at her request and, like Bill Pinar's move above. Ming and Bill Schubert asked me to consider their series in IAP for the edited book that became *Sensuous Curriculum: Politics and the Senses in Education* (Gershon, 2019).

Feeling someone who has just heard the music swell as they try to thank everyone during an awards show, I've all but run out of the room I've been given and am not close to finished. I need to thank Noreen Garman, Bill Doll, Joanne Dowdy, Tom Barone, Janet Miller, Todd Price, Anna Wilson, Peter Appelbaum, Patti Lather, Ming Fang He, Bill Schubert, Deb Freedman, Will Letts, Jim Sears, Bettie St. Pierre, Bill Ayers, Erica Meiners, Dave Stovall, Therese Quinn, Warren Critchlow, and so many others who nurtured this weird nugget of a scholar I've become. Rob Helfenbein, Kent den Heyer, Boni Wozolek, and Reagan Mitchell are friends and confidants without whom I don't think I could have made it, really. Last but not least, I am particularly grateful for so many of my colleagues whom I've "grown up" with and sad I've run out of room to name them all. Please know I mean you.

References

Bresler, L. (1995). The subservient, co-equal, affective, and social integration styles and their implications for the arts, *Arts Education Policy Review*, 96(5), 31–37.

82 Walter Gershon

Bresler, L. (1998). Research, policy, and practice in arts education: Meeting points for conversation. *Arts Education Policy Review, 99*(5), 9–15.

Bull, M., & Back, L. (Eds.). (2004). *The auditory culture reader.* Oxford: Berg.

Drobnick, J. (Ed.). (2004). *Audio cultures.* Toronto: YYZ.

Erlmann, V. (2004). *Hearing cultures: Essays on sound, listening, and modernity.* New York, NY: Routledge.

Feld, S. (1982). *Sound and sentiment: Birds, weeping, poetics, and song in Kaluli expression.* Philadelphia, PA: University of Pennsylvania Press.

Feld, S., & Basso, K. H. (Eds.). (1996). *Senses of place.* Santa Fe, NM: School of American Research Press.

Feld, S., & Brenneis, D. (2004). Doing anthropology in sound. *American Ethnologist, 31*(4), 461–474.

Gershon, W. S. (2017). *Sound Curriculum: Sonic studies in educational theory, method, and practice.* New York, NY: Routledge.

Gershon, W. S. (2019). *Sensuous curriculum: Politics and the senses in education.* Charlotte, NC: IAP.

Howes, D. (Ed.). (1991). *The varieties of sensory experience: A sourcebook in the anthropology of the senses.* Toronto: University of Toronto Press.

Howes, D. (2003). *Sensual relations: Engaging the senses in culture & social theory.* Ann Arbor, MI: University of Michigan Press.

Howes, D. (Ed.) (2005). *Empire of the senses: The sensual culture reader* (pp. 179–191). Oxford: Berg Press.

Pinar, W. F., & Irwin, R. L. (2005). *Curriculum in a new key: The collected works of Ted T. Aoki.* Mahwah, NJ: Lawrence Erlbaum.

Powell, K. (2006). Inside-out and outside-in: Participant observation in Taiko drumming. In G. Spindler & L. Hammond (Eds.), *Innovations in educational ethnography: Theory, methods, and results* (pp. 33–64). Mahwah, NJ: Lawrence Erlbaum.

Price, R., & Price, S. (1991). *Two evenings in Saramaka.* Chicago, IL: University of Chicago Press.

Rascher, S. M. (1968). *158 saxophone exercises.* New York, NY: G. Schirmer, Inc.

Sterne, J. (2003). *The audible past: Cultural origins of sound reproduction.* Cambridge, MA: MIT Press.

Stoller, P. (1989). *The taste of ethnographic things: The senses in anthropology.* Philadelphia, PA: University of Pennsylvania Press.

Stoller, P. (1997). *Sensuous scholarship.* Philadelphia, PA: University of Pennsylvania Press.

Wozolek, B. (2021). *Assemblages of violence in education: Everyday trajectories of oppression.* New York, NY: Routledge.

9 The Butterfly Catcher

Kathryn Ricketts

Intermingling Souls

In the Fall of 1981, I was propelled off Simon Fraser University's (SFU) main stage with excitement and relief, confident that I would be a performer for life! I had never felt such crystallized intensity and knew that this experience would have long-lasting resonations. Despite the deeply poetic implications of the piece I had just performed, they were left in the wake of my own narcissistic effervescence. The fact that we were dancing an immigrant's story of arrival and departure, of place and displacement, of identity and heritage, ancestry and roots, seemed to pass me by. Elitist narcissism obsessed with physical virtuosity is often the location of a dancer and I am troubled to admit, I was not exempt from this. For many years with varying degrees of authenticity and depth, this was my world of dance until...an important interruption.

I arrived at a dance studio in Copenhagen at the age of 28 to meet my long-standing friend, soon to forge through a very difficult journey that forever shaped my directions as an artist, scholar, and educator. His exotic Columbian imagination soon found a complement in my seemingly unusual ways of seeing the world and we began to collaborate ALL the time. Portable cassette player under the arm, we imposed our kinaesthetic machinations on the general public anywhere, anytime! We built a repertoire of performances for just the two of us and large groups, both in theatres, rough studios, back allies, on busy streets, and rooftops.

Now I was called to be at his side during his last years suffering from AIDS. He was one of the first generations to die of AIDS with only rudimentary drugs in place to prolong the imminent outcome. I was there as an extension of his body, a conduit for his wild imagination and an amplifier to his dancers who eagerly awaited the completion of a show he had already started before becoming very ill.

We undoubtedly had intermingling souls and thus his expressions and invitations to movement were easily caught by me like a delicate net catching exotic butterflies. I transformed these "butterflies" into

DOI: 10.4324/9781003154112-10

84   Kathryn Ricketts

movement, which in turn were interpreted and transformed yet again by the dancers who were eagerly poised before me.

For 18 months of my life, I became the creative and kinaesthetic channel for my friend with AIDS. While he was dying, I was living fervently, double time, and in doing this my world of dance radically shifted as my body became purely the access point for him. I had been present for my first dying process and recognized the terrible beauty in this journey, potent with creativity and combined with an almost acidic lucidity. The vitality in this crisis where imagination lacked the compliment of a body; using another body as a vehicle for his voice, was profoundly transformational. This radically shifted my position as dancer/artist to a focus of uncovering stories of others through movement and allowing this in turn to be a catalyst for shared empathy within a community.

> Lynn Fels (1998) helped me to define this method I was exploring, as performative inquiry as she so eloquently describes: "Transported into an unexpected environment, the student must re-examine the familiar against the unfamiliar, and through the resulting disequilibrium recover a new balance of meeting oneself within a new environment." (p.12)

What follows are memories of the poignant moments in my work with my dear friend and how they have shaped me as a scholar, performer and teacher today in relation to Curriculum Development and Performance Studies.

I owned the door!

I had lived half of my day by the time he arose from his long and meandering night of sleep and sleeplessness. Cigarettes extinguished in half empty yogurt containers and random selections of pages torn from stacks of *all* the books rifled through in desperate search for distraction.

I had cycled, ran, made art, visited the local Danish bakery and was waiting for his emergence from the darkened bedroom of the grand villa where we lived together. Then there was the silent slow immersion into the day where I needed to be present but somewhat invisible. The visitors would be arriving soon at our front door of which *I* owned. It was I that mitigated the constant parade of gem holders, feather wavers, and ointment spreaders. All in goodwill to "heal" my friend who was minding his own business and dying of AIDS.

For this performative task I understood the costuming was paramount. Black leather jacket (even on the hottest days), blood-red lipstick, and bleached blonde spikey short hair. I was the "bitch from Canada" who efficiently kept this man from the *possibility of miracles*. The shell I built protected the soft parts only reserved for him. This performative necessity has informed how I navigate the balance between agency and humility, especially within the complexity of the academy.

The Monkeys Asked, I Answered

He would be waiting from his bed when I returned excited and overheated from dance rehearsal. My job was to finish the show he had started, to elongate his brilliant choreographic voice, his surreal Columbian imagination, across town to a large studio with five dancers who waited eagerly to be shown the next move towards *his* ingenuity. His collection of stuffed monkeys, his elected and primary representatives, Pufi and Rocco, were in the lead and all would be lined up on the bed and waiting with bated breath to hear about the day's rehearsal, and who said what?, and how did she take that? and how many cigarettes did they smoke on break? etc.

The monkeys asked, I answered and the dying man smiled and nodded with great satisfaction.

Image 9.1 Jorge and Pafi Photo and collage by Jorge Holguin Copenhagen, Denmark 1985

86 *Kathryn Ricketts*

At times we got so excited we would make rap songs about the challenges of the rehearsal on a tiny Fisher-Price speaker and microphone system. Then it was my turn to ask the monkeys how *their* day was. There were reports of fevers and diarrhoea, rashes and coughs. And sometimes they would reveal a most minuscule fear that would slip out of the corner of their furry mouths.

This line up of plush translators and the ridiculous amplification of the Fisher-Price speaker system taught me how to navigate the complexity of voices that need to be heard through the most unexpected means. Voices that hide under beds and in closets and need to be coaxed out in ways I had never imagined. Marjorie Seigel (1995) talks about transmediation and the necessary transfer from one medium of information to another and the syntax that occurs affording a generative and innovative meaning making. Dorothy Heathcote (1984) referred to

> ...the principle of "ostranenie" defined by Viktor Shklovsky as being "that of making strange." We very readily cease to "see" the world we live in and become anaesthetized to its distinctive features. The arts permit us "to reverse that process and to creatively deform the usual, the normal, and so to inculcate a new, childlike, non-jaded vision in us".
>
> (p. 127)

Blood Transfusions

Every week had its own rhythm
We were tightly tethered to haemoglobin counts
The transfusions were regular and frequent
and dictated the energy, the possibilities for outings.

The question was "Could he come to rehearsal that day?"
The answer was "Yes for two days after the infusion."

Sitting up against the mirror of the dance studio wrapped in a blanket
Me, listening to the carefully chosen words cloaked in tone and nuance
    of expression
Tumbling through my body to the dancers
Speaking back in a dialogue three times removed
This is how we made the dance of his life.

> ...These are all demanding activities, requiring the use of perception, imagination, speculation, and interpretation, as well as exercising dramatic, cognitive, and social capacities. These capacities and the energies of the group are focused on the development of

The Butterfly Catcher   87

a specific dramatic world arising from a particular pre-text that defines the parameters of this world.

(O'Neil & Lambert, 1982, p.1)

My Theory of BIGNESS – Ordinary Meets Extraordinary

I complained of his style, (we still argued regularly; it somehow kept us grounded), "Your style is so BIG it is like having cheese sandwich with cheese." He challenged my viewpoint "Prove to me your theory of Bigness against smallness." On the programme with his finished piece I submitted a very small piece call *Lester*. A very tall man sits on a very small wooden chair in his bathrobe. He is eating a bowl of cereal perfectly timed to the musical accompaniment of Pomp and Circumstance. Every crescendo is met with either an unenthusiastic spoonful of soggy cereal or an irritated wiggle and checking of the seat of the chair.

The final crescendo results in Lester pulling a hammer out of his bathrobe pocket and the tentative taps at a nail that has been disturbing his morning meal. Two slides go up on the screen behind Lester to complete the piece. The first slide gives the definition of ordinary as uninteresting or commonplace. The second slide asks True or False?

We seemed to find the extraordinary gift of life every day in the small daily rituals together in his last year. I learned to continue this throughout my life, to think of the soggy cereal and the little nail and the hammer in the pocket, all within the grandeur of our living moment to moment. These moments are fleeting and work *through* the form we present like an express train as Fels (1998) stated "The edge of chaos is the balancing point between order and chaos..." (p. 257)

The Final Field Trip

The monkeys had their big outing on a summer day in 1989. The lineup was moved from the bed to the inside of the coffin huddled up against Jorge protectively. They were silent but fierce and I knew all the stories and secrets they held and smiled down on them as I passed by towards the pew. I kept my eye on my new shoes throughout the service hoping that they may save my grief from rattling around the floors and banging at the windows.

Outside in the shade, I stood awaiting the transfer from the church to the hearse, around the corner came six strong men struggling with their task but not from the weight, nor the narrow passage but from the lineup of furry creatures, Rocco and Pafi in the lead, precariously balanced in a row on the lid of the coffin. If it wasn't for my heart breaking in two I would have doubled over with glee as I watched the parade of creatured ambassadors teeter and rock as they clung to the

88 Kathryn Ricketts

Image 9.2 "Lester" Photographer – Jens Hemmel Dancer – Christian Holland Copenhagen, Denmark 1988

lid through the difficult journey into the hearse. The sombre black vehicle moved very, very slowly and I did not envy the poor driver, sweat on his brow as he kept his eyes glued on the rear-view mirror and his precarious guests.

Rocco and Pafi are with me now and make their appearances diligently and loyally in every class I teach as they tell their story of giving Jorge his voice in the last year of his life. Sometimes we need monkeys....

As enormously difficult as this was, heart-wrenching really, it was a gift I will cherish forever as Jorge taught me how to access my dancing

The Butterfly Catcher   89

body as a butterfly net for the stories of others and the stories that need to be told but are silenced or muffled.

Certeau (as cited in Conquergood, 2002, p. 145) wrote that "what the map cuts up, the story cuts across," by looking at different domains of knowledge and how these domains, the story and the dance, the theory and the practice, can create tensions of understanding. Conquergood in his quote of Certeau writes of this tension as what sits at the heart of Performance Studies

> ...transgressive travel between two different domains of knowledge: one official, objective, and abstract – "the map"; the other one practical, embodied, and popular – "the story." This promiscuous traffic between different ways of knowing carries the most radical promise of performance studies research. Performance studies struggles to open the space between analysis and action, and to pull the pin of the binary opposition between theory and practice.
>
> (Conquergood, 2002, p.145)

This form of abstraction helps to transport the story from specifics (i.e., character, setting, context) to personal and then to a shared platform with others inviting personal lived experiences to emerge as invitations to creative participatory and collective meaning making. "Most significantly, these activities illuminate the processes by which human beings experience a sense of personal identity and, importantly, how these experiences are necessarily organized by remembered, currently lived, and imagined identifications and relationships." (Sumara, 2001, p. 168)

Heathcote (1984) wrote about drama as the construction of and the invitation to "another room" (p. 129). This room allows for the possibility of dissolving the practicalities and pragmatics of time, space, and consequence and for the merging of performer and spectator. Heathcote (1984) describes this as a "no-penalty" zone (p. 129) and this space allows us to actually see the world opposed to merely recognizing it.

This experience with Jorge was directly tethered to subsequent graduate work where I fell into a community of arts-based scholars who enabled an articulation in sound theories and practices. I studied with vibrant scholars from the University of British Columbia (UBC) where I could steep my curiosities in A/r/tography (Springgay, Irwin, Leggo, & Gouzouasis, 2008), Performative Inquiry (Fels, 1998) and then later at SFU where I worked within embodied ways of knowing (Snowber, 2007) and phenomenology (Smith, 2017). With this kaleidoscopic journey of mentored scholarship, I was able to define a method that I coin as Embodied Poetic Narrative. This trilogy allows narratives, objects of meaning, and bodily expression to co-mingle and allow voice to be shared and heard within a co-constructed community. I was able to take

Image 9.3 "In the Midst" Photograher – Kim Ernest Dancers – Kathryn Ricketts, Jorge Holguin Copenhagen, Denmark 1988

this forward with my passion to resuscitate voice within disenfranchised communities such as I did with Jorge in the studio long ago.

To this end, I am currently working as the Director of Innovative Educative Practices and Field Experience in the Faculty of Education at the University of Regina. In this role, I try to mend, fortify, and enliven the relationships between our education intern students, teachers in the field, and our faculty advisors who support their internships. This facilitation may seem far away from the butterfly net in the studio in Copenhagen but I see the dancer diligently and carefully catching the stories and expressions that need to be caught, heard, and appreciated.

I will always be grateful for the gift of this opportunity with my dear friend Jorge who taught me how to catch butterflies and for the scholars both of UBC and SFU Faculties of Education who polished and refined this gift until it could refract and reflect with power and impact for the rest of my time as a performing, facilitating, and educating scholar.

References

Conquergood, D. (2002). Performance studies: Interventions and radical research. *The Drama Review*, 46(2), 145–156.

The Butterfly Catcher 91

Fels, L. (1998). *In the wind clothes dance on a line performative inquiry: A (re) search methodology (Unpublished* doctoral dissertation). University of British Columbia, Vancouver, British Columbia, Canada.

Heathcote, D. (1984). *Drama in the curriculum: Material for significance.* Evansten, IL: Northwestern University Press.

O'Neil, C., & Lambert, A. (1982). *Drama structure: A practical handbook for teachers.* London: Hutchinson Education.

Siegel, M. (1995). More than words: The power of transmediation for learning. *Canadian Journal of Education, Toronto, 20*(4), 455–475.

Smith, S.J. (2017). The vitality of humanimality: From the perspective of life phenomenology. *Phenomenology & Practice, 11*(1), 72–88.

Snowber, C. (2007). The soul moves: Dance and spirituality in educative practice. In L. Bresler (Ed.), *International handbook for research in the arts and education* (pp. 1449–1458). Dordrecht, Germany: Springer.

Springgay, S., Irwin, R.L., Leggo, C., & Gouzouasis, P. (Eds.). (2008). *Being with A/r/tography.* Rotterdam: Sense Publishers.

Sumara, D.J. (2001). Learning to create insight: Literary engagements as purposeful pedagogy. *Changing English, 8*(2), 165–175.

10 Aporias

Geo-metrons Sounding in the Silence of the Void

Patricia Palulis

Jacques Derrida, in the preamble to his Aporias, makes reference to a welcoming grace [*grâce prévenante*]. The call for proposals ignites my affinities for the French poststructuralists – for the exquisite intensities of language when Derrida alerts us to spacing praxis in his magnificent *Glas*: "Let us space" – a hospitable invitation into experiential writing that moves without knowing destination "*en accolant et en décollant*" (Derrida, 1986, p. 75) – a doubling to create the tensions of writing outside the templates of the Land of Academia. Mentors in their giftings become entangled with one another. I draw from Ted Aoki's geo-metrons as *survivance* – as soundscapes of lived experience in everyday life. West coast Aokian geo-metrons chiming, shimmering, trembling, crackling as words step off the page and out the door into the circulation of city life in the nation's capital. Aoki always reminded us that the void was a space of generative possibilities – that lack was an open space rich with possibilities. I want to share these legacies with my students at the University of Ottawa.

Students respond with exquisite languaging. Cultural, spiritual and ecological traces thread their journeys into spatial praxis to unsettle the dust – to disrupt erupt rupture. There are those who resist and I struggle in the tensioned spaces hoping that generative possibilities will emerge. Walking with words in the nation's capital to protest injustices, words step off the page to soundscapes of radical demonstration *en route* and on Parliament Hill. *Survivance* in the nation's capital. Words step out the door chanting echoing refrains from one protest to another – in the wind and the rain. I have often encountered my students en route as we join the protest.

I am grateful for the timeliness of a book arrival as I write and am written in this chapter: "Contemporary Voices from Anima Mundi A Reappraisal" edited by Frederique Apffel-Marglin and Stefano Varese. When you need a respite from human contact, Anima Mundi takes you into the gift and grace of spirituality. An exquisite reminder of my participation in the Bio-cultural Re-generation Institute attended in the Summer of 2013 (Palulis, 2018). Varese teaches us that the spirits of

DOI: 10.4324/9781003154112-11

Aporias   93

sacred plants heal the world. Apffel-Marglin teaches us about integrated pedagogy and the powers of ecospirituality. This gift emerged from the friendship of Pat O'Riley and Peter Cole on the West Coast who told me to hop on a plane and come down to join them at Sachamama in Peru. I am grateful to them and to Frederique for an amazing experience that challenged my comfort zone. The smudging by a shaman as a cloak of protection has been lingering with me for the times when I need the remembering for shelter and comfort.

On a bookshelf at the Sachamama Biocultural Regeneration Institute in the Summer of 2013, I found a book authored by Karen Barad. I seek Barad's entanglements in a posthuman world. I want Peter Cole's and Pat O'Riley's resistance to the rituals of templates. To see their performance of Coyote and Raven is a gift. I am grateful that we are friends. I am grateful to my mentors for opening new worlds. I struggle most with the concept of a "welcoming grace" – how to continue to welcome when the going gets rough. Derrida writes of an (un)conditional welcoming to the stranger – without needing from the stranger a name. How can we continue the work and the words that he bequeathed to us? Let us space, he said. Let the space be open to welcoming the stranger. What happens when the neighbour becomes the stranger? Ted Aoki who was born in Canada is interned in a camp after the Japanese entered the Second World War. And when the stranger becomes the neighbour, generative possibilities emerge for contributing to community. The story of a Syrian opening a chocolate shop in Nova Scotia offering employment to local people. A "welcoming grace" continues to give a gift. I want to belong to the group that says "No one is illegal" and continues to respect the indigenous inhabitants of the land. I am attentive to the geo-metrons sounding for Gaza: *From the river to the sea, Palestina will be free.* We chant in the wind and in the rain on Parliament Hill.

On lockdown, how can we continue the resistance, disobedience, blasphemy? How can we release the words to perform the work for social justice? With the self-isolation of lockdown, the memories of hometown life seep through the silence of the void. The longing for returns are shattered as be/longing is out of reach. An old narrative simply repeats itself. Looking for home in all the wrong places, I am now searching for fragments. Home is sometimes found in a fragment of text, in the bark of a birch tree, in a lady-slipper, in a butter-cup, in a purple violet, with a speckled trout in a fast-running brook, on the pathway up blueberry hill. Perhaps in a photo or a postcard. But not in the lived experience of a childhood of never belonging to a hometown. I finally realize that the "not" belonging was what may have motivated me to seek out endless paths of new adventures. At a High School reunion, a friend asked me: How did you know there was an outside? At that time, the only way out was by train. The Algoma Central Railway – offered the first segment of the journey out. A gift. And then the pathways opened up to endless

94 Patricia Palulis

possibilities: to volcanic sea stacks in the Faroe Islands, to snowstorms in the Arctic, to icebergs and ice floes off the coast of Greenland. To sandstorms in the Sahara. I remember with gratitude the Tuaregs driving us in their jeeps over sand dunes in the Sahara so that we might view a magnificent sunset. I am still grateful that the camels were all booked and none were available to us. I rode on a camel around the pyramids in Egypt. No. More. Camels.

To volcanoes and lava flows in Iceland. I remember climbing the summit of the dormant volcano Thrihnukagigur to experience the descent into the magma chamber. A harpist and a folksinger accompanied us and staged a concert for us inside the magma chamber of the volcano. Memories are gifts. On a boat tour in the south of Iceland we enter a volcanic water cave and the guide begins to play his saxophone for us there in the watery cave with the blurring of purple and green and blue hues on the volcanic walls of the cave. Geo-metrons sounding in landscapes. I am seeking Icelandic children's books and at a studio shop in the old harbour, I am offered a chance to meet an Icelandic author/artist and her American co-author. Gunnella invites me to her studio. Entanglements take me on new adventures and I am grateful.

What happens to us as we take leave from a creative experience at our home university and take a position in a templated existence? How can we spiral backwards in order to move forward? Through resistance, disobedience, blasphemy, and refusal. I am inspired by indigenous authors to continue as an ally in their movement. I am grateful to the authors proposing a third space, a third discourse, spaces of hybridity that open to generative possibilities. I am grateful that I had the opportunity to take a summer course taught by Ted Aoki at the University of British Columbia (UBC). A three-week course that changed my life, opening up new worlds of possibility that I had not known existed. We were introduced to third space through the work of Homi K. Bhabha and Trinh T. Minh-ha. During the past few years in Ottawa, I have had a chance to hear both Trinh and Bhabha make presentations. Trinh was in Montreal for the event of her art installation. We were staying in the same B&B and were checking out at the same time. I introduced myself as a longtime groupie of hers and she gave me a hug. Bhabha gave a mesmerizing presentation at Carleton University. Friends came from Montreal and we attended the event together. Bhabha shook hands with us as we lingered following the event. Ted Aoki was there in spirit looking over my shoulder with me as I attended to the authors and the words that he had shared with us.

My gratitude extends to Anthropology Professor Elvi Whittaker for continuing to mentor me after I took her critical ethnography course at UBC. I had wanted the challenge of having someone on my dissertation committee who was outside the Faculty of Education. I was so very grateful later to be invited to submit a chapter in a book that she was editing. Her feminist approach was performed through her welcoming

Aporias 95

grace as she invited each of us to read and comment on all the chapters in the book. I was in Iceland at the time writing with excitement about elves and their habitats in volcanic landscapes when the invitation arrived. The elves are still waiting their turn for a space and place in my storytelling. One day soon, I have promised them.

I locate a chapter written by Jacques Mabit (2020) in the edited book by Apffel-Marglin (2020) and Varese (2020). Mabit brings the Sorcerer, the Madman and Grace together in Amazonian shamanism as a return "to the body and to the earth" (p. 145). I have yet to experience ayahuasca, the vision-inducing plant of the central Amazon region, for "the controlled inducement of altered states of awareness" (p. 145). I hope to return someday to Sachamama and will seek out the possibility of this experience. Through altered states of awareness, Mabit speaks of vertical and horizontal integration with ancestors and contemporaries. Aoki spoke of verticality and horizontality in a "third" discourse. Soundscapes as geo-metrons become entangled in the silence of the void. Silence resonates with generative possibilities.

I have struggled most with the concept of "grace" as a *grâce prévenante* seems to be lacking in the everyday life of Academia. I seem to have fallen from grace in my templated existence in the Land of Academia. A falling from grace with the Madman. A seeking of grace from the Sorcerer. As I am falling from grace, I seek refuge in the words of indigenous scholars who acknowledge that we must bite the hand that feeds us (Tuck, 2018) and we must refuse the university (Grande, 2018). Drawing from, Grande bypasses resistance for the power of refusal which "throws into doubt the entire system and is therefore more dangerous" (p. 181). She refers to "love as refusal" as "the un-demand, the un-desire to be *of* or *in*" (p. 184). Rather "it is the radical assertion to be *on* land" (p. 184). I have come to realize that the gifts of memories are often related to the landscapes on which the stories took place. *On* land. Reconnecting us to our relationship and responsibility to the land. On the tundra in the Canadian Arctic, on the pathways through the old-growth forests of the West Coast, on the foothills of Fuji-san in Japan, on the desert sands of the Sahara, on the lava fields of Iceland, on the pathways of the Amazonian rainforests of Peru. Geo-metrons *on* land.

Mignolo (2011) evokes epistemic disobedience. We are called upon to risk "danger" in the Land of Academia. One reads a pathway into writing slowly cautiously fearfully hopefully seeking an escape from the templates of Academia and then quietly and unobtrusively words begin to seep out from the cracks. Aoki used a diagonal slash to crack words wide open for generative possibilities to emerge – for newness to emerge. His legacy is living on.

Gratitude extends to the difficult spaces and times. Writing is always in the context of a circulating lived experience. Lebanon is suffering. How can the concept of a welcoming grace [*grâce prévenante*] extend

96 *Patricia Palulis*

our love and our help to the people of Lebanon? I am watching through the window as raindrops share the sorrow of weeping. A gifting of rain to perform the sorrow. I am grateful. I remember a doubling performance of a visual artist painting on a screen and a musician playing his clarinet in exquisite sorrow for their homeland of Syria. I was unable to attend another performance in the Ottawa chamber music festival as I was so immersed in the remembrance of that concert. Perhaps the geo-metrons of exquisite sorrow are a gifting of soundscapes to what Derrida (1993) has described as a doubling in a "strange topography of edges" (p. 80). I am grateful to the shaman for the protection of smudging as I dwell within the everyday tensions of Academia. Aporias evoke the tensions in the doublings of (im)possibilities.

Geo-metrons are sounding in the textual terrains of a multiplicity of landscapes. When I find myself nested in the welcoming grace and warmth of hospitality, I am grateful. I am reading Claudia Ruitenberg (2016) reading Derrida on the ethic of hospitality. How can we work towards an ethic of hospitality in the Land of Academia? Welcoming our students into a doubling space of pedagogical (im)possibilities. Welcoming our faculty colleagues into richly textured conversations. Learning to in-dwell with the tensions.

My gratitude extends to the invitation to be included in this inspirational collection of papers. I am grateful to the editors for their welcoming grace [*grâce prévenante*] and for this gift.

References

Apffel-Marglin, F. (2020). Western modernity and the fate of anima mundi. In F. Apffel-Marglin & S. Varese (Eds.), *Contemporary voices from anima mundi: A reappraisal* (pp. 17–44). New York, NY: Peter Lang.

Derrida, J. (1993) *Aporias*. Trans. Tomas Dutoit. Stanford, CA: Stanford University Press.

Derrida, J. (1986). *Glas*. Trans. John P. Leavey, Jr. and Richard Rand. Lincoln and London: University of Nebraska Press.

Grande, S. (2018). Refusing the university. In Marc Spooner & James McNinch (Eds.), *Dissident knowledge in higher education* (pp. 168–189). Regina: University of Regina Press.

Mabit, J. (2020). The sorcerer, the madman and grace. In F. Apffel-Marglin & S. Varese (Eds.), *Contemporary voices from anima mundi: A reappraisal* (pp. 113–154). New York, NY: Peter Lang.

Mignolo, W. (2011). Epistemic disobedience and the decolonial option: A manifesto. *TRANSMODERNITY: Journal of Peripheral Cultural Production of the Luso-Hispanic World, 1*(2), 44–67.

Palulis P. (2018) Black Earth green Moon Mama Allpa: Polyphonic moments from temple to tambo. In G. Reis & J. Scott (Eds.) *International perspectives on the theory and practice of environmental education: A reader*. Environmental Discourses in Science Education, vol 3. Cham: Springer.

Ruitenberg, C. (2016). *Unlocking the world: Education in an ethic of hospitality*. New York, NY: Routledge.

Tuck, E. (2018). Biting the university that feeds us. In Marc Spooner and James McNinch (eds.) *Dissident knowledge in higher education*. Regina: University of Regina Press. 149–167.

Varese, S. (2020). Between matter and spirit: An unfinished journey. In F. Apffel-Marglin & S. Varese (Eds.), *Contemporary voices from anima mundi: A reappraisal* (pp. 155–180). New York, NY: Peter Lang.

11 Dear Carl

A Letter of Gratitude for the Gifts of Education

Graham W. Lea

Introduction

I was fortunate to have a 'dream team' committee for my doctoral research project *Homa Bay Memories: Using Research-based Theatre to Explore a Narrative Inheritance* (2013). Drs. George Belliveau (2018), Rita Irwin (2013), and Carl Leggo (2017) each brought unique and valuable insights based on their decades of experience forging the way for arts-based research. Their guidance helped me grow as a scholar and a person. In 2019, it became clear that Carl's time on Earth was coming to a close. Wanting to express my gratitude for his impacts on my life, I wrote him a letter which, unfortunately, he was never able to read. The following is an adapted version of that letter.

•••

Dear Carl,

I begin with the only thing I think we can begin with, a story.

Recently I was teaching an 8:30 am class on a very cold Manitoba morning. Being a person who enjoys neither the morning nor the cold, I was not in a very enthusiastic frame of mind as students filed into the classroom removing layers upon layers of winter garments that protected them from the cold. Many had coffee cups in their hands. Some looked energized and ready to start the day, others looked like they could have slept until noon. While others mingled, a few students set up our usual circle of chairs. We all sat in the circle and began as we often do, with a check-in.

But something tugged at my sleeve, as Lynn would say (Fels, 2012).

Responses began with the typical student comments around being stressed and overworked. Comments that, while valuable, put a damper on the energy of the room. About halfway through the circle a young woman dealing with mobility issues in her arms spoke. She said how grateful she was for the students who set up the chairs first thing in the morning.

DOI: 10.4324/9781003154112-12

Dear Carl 99

TUG.

Gratitude. Such an important practice. One I don't engage in frequently enough.

I listened to that student. That teacher. For in that moment she was indeed my teacher. I listened beyond her words. She was guiding me as I internally grumbled about the cold.

I stopped the activity.

We started again. This time I asked students to share something for which they were grateful.

I started with the student on my left – I told myself I did so to not influence students' thinking.

Responses ran the gamut:

Family
Pets
Coffee
Mobility
Cars that start
Legs that could feel the cold

Some were serious. Some were silly. But all were grateful.

In truth, it took me the whole circle to reframe my cold, dark, wintery mindset to find something I was grateful for. But I did.

That was the lesson. It wasn't for the circle; it wasn't for the class. It was for me.

What am I grateful for?

How do I express it?

I have continued this gratitude circle periodically in other classes. Perhaps someday I might even have the courage to suggest doing it at a department meeting. But I am sure you can imagine how a room full of academics might respond to that!

Is this something new? No, of course not. But it is something important. It is an important reminder to me.

Gratitude.

Gratefulness.

Often we wait too long, don't get the chance to express our deep gratitude to those who have impacted our lives.

Carl, Thank You.

Your words, your way of being in the world, has been one of the great influences on my early academic career, particularly in the classroom.

I never had the chance to take a course from you, something I heard a colleague once describe as an "academic spa." But seeing your presence in the world and hearing from others about your classes helped

100   Graham W. Lea

shape my approach to working with people beginning their pedagogic journeys.

One of the courses I teach focuses on integrating the arts across the curriculum, a mandatory course for everyone intending to teach in the early and middle years (that this is not required for those intending to teach senior years is a thorn in my side).

When I was assigned the course, I became quite nervous. How could I teach these students to integrate all of the art forms in just 36 short hours?

> I work in drama, I know some skills, yet there is still so much
> I don't know, ...
> I am not a visual artist, yet they need to know painting, sketching,
> sculpture, ...
> I am not a dancer, yet they need to know movement, dance, how
> to exist in space, ...
> I am not a musician, yet they need to know winds, strings, brass,
> choral, ...

I came to realize that was not the point. The course can't prepare all teachers to be *art teachers*, nor should it. Nor can it teach people to be *artists*. Many have not seen their artistic sides in many, many years.

There needed to be some theory on art integration, for sure. But more than that it needed to be a place of exploration, of (re)discovery, of (re)understanding and coming to know their *artistic selves*.

One of the major course assignments I developed is to create an artist/ teacher portfolio of multiple artworks in various artforms. I encourage students to reflect on their emerging pedagogic identities and how the artmaking processes might reflect that. Like the gratitude circle, students come to the task with differing levels of commitment, but it is always fascinating to see how the class comes together as they share their artworks and learnings with each other.

> Paintings
> Ceramics
> Dance
> Poetry
> I even had one document the recreation of a car transmission!
> Some very personal
> Some very detached
> All meaningful

Carl, Thank You.

> Without observing and hearing about your way of being, I would
> not have had the courage to engage in this approach to teaching.

Dear Carl 101

But it wasn't just your work in the classroom for which I am grateful; I was so very fortunate to have you as a member of my doctoral committee.

While dissertating (or disintegrating, or perhaps both), I found several times that I could not express the ideas I wanted to share in either academic prose or the theatre script that formed the heart of the dissertation.

Their voices bounce back and forth
Blending and building over the checkered Starbucks table

Slouched in a soft brown leather chair
I look up from my reading

Was it Bakhtin or maybe Dewey?

They disappear into inaudible stories

Living stories
Evolving stories
Tied together

Travelling on waves in all directions
Through the air
Through other stories
Tangling with mine

Across the room
Wisps of hair escape her tightly bound ponytail
As she reads
Her silent story
Tangling with mine

While Bakhtin or Dewey sits dead in my lap

(Lea, 2013, p. 18)

With you as a committee member, I felt comfortable pushing myself. I wrote what I referred to in my defence as poem-lets.

> Small collections of words that follow no rules other than the innate sense of when they were put together correctly.

You never dismissed from your poet's chair. You saw value in them, if to no one else but me.

102 *Graham W. Lea*

Moon's gift to the waves

a lone wave flashes
disappearing into blackness

together they twinkle
carpeting the ocean in a corridor of light

how odd, when you think of it, this miracle of light!

how odd, when you think of it, this miracle of light
exploding from infinite closeness
struggling thousands of years to breach the sun
bouncing from moon to dance on black-water waves before
imbedding itself in my pupil.

Moon's gift to the waves
I gift to you

(Lea, 2013, p. 196)

Carl, Thank You.

I could not have written them without you.

Have I kept it up, made poem-lets a practice? No. Perhaps, I still carry too much self-doubt, self-shame, insecurity.

My transition from student to academic was not as smooth as I might have hoped. Circumstances in my personal and professional life conspired to shake my already shaky sense of self.

On one of those days, I called you.
I am sure there was a pretext for doing so.
Perhaps career advice
Perhaps publishing something
I don't remember why I called.
Nor do I remember most of the conversation.
I guess it really didn't matter.
But I remember the feeling.
You heard beyond the pretext
You heard the self-doubt
You heard the self-shame
You heard the insecurity

Your words were ones of support, of encouragement.
They were a positive light in what seemed a dark world.

What I do clearly remember saying to you "I wish I had your voice in my head."

Dear Carl 103

But perhaps I did – and still do. Bakhtin's (1986) notion of chains of utterances suggests that we exist within webs of continuous inter-relationships, that the self is dependent on the other/others for its construction. Our identity is shaped not just by ourselves but also in the perceptions of others, some of which are unknowable to us. This "excess of seeing" (Bakhtin, 1990; Fenske, 2004), or "surplus of seeing" (Holquist, 2002) may be thought of as 'what I see of you that you cannot and what you see of me that I cannot.' As I recall your voice, your presence, I create a "finalization (form-bestowing activity) [which] does not close down possibilities as much as produce a space of encounter with life/living" (Fenske, 2004, p. 10). As I recall you, your words, I create an opportunity to engage with your surplus of seeing and by doing so see new reflections of myself.

The beauty of having known you is that I do and always will. I just have to remember to listen for it.

Carl, Thank You.

Your kind words and voice still reverberate in my head creating new frequencies of my being.

After I completed my dissertation, I met you in your office. It was one of the few one-on-one meetings we ever had. Surrounded by your books, we talked for a long time.

It was there, with the dissertation completed, the defence defended, the uploads uploaded, that I finally began to understand what I was doing with my work.

In our conversation, you guided me to a discovery, one much more profound, much more meaningful than any written in the pages of that text.

You helped me see that my dissertation was not a study of education in international contexts across time as it was originally intended. Nor was it even a study of a son, trying to learn about his mother's teaching experiences in Kenya and by doing so understand his narrative inheritance (Goodall, 2006) and how that shaped him as a teacher. It wasn't even an examination of research-based theatre methodology.

It was a spiritual process. It was my coming to the understanding that while my mother may not live in the physical world she continues to live on inside me, in the waves her stories leave in my stories. And by understanding her in this way I could get to know her in new ways across the borders of time, place, and mortality.

Carl, Thank You.

You helped me begin to understand a spiritual side to myself I thought I had pushed away.

You allowed me a space as a member of my committee, and as a pioneer in artful ways of engaging in research, to write a phrase that has guided much of my personal and professional lives since:

104 Graham W. Lea

"We are nothing but the waves our stories leave in the stories of others" (Lea, 2013, p. 21).

I am so grateful to have worked with you, to have known you. I am so grateful your stories have influenced mine. I hope that in time, those waves you have left in my stories, will leave similar waves in the stories of some of my students.

Dear Carl, this letter is addressed to you, but it contains a message to everyone I have encountered on my formal and informal pedagogical journeys: Rita, George, my mother, the grateful student in the circle, even my grade 2/3 teacher whose approach to teaching was so dated that my young mind decided to rebel and as a result I have been a math teacher who can't multiply and an English teacher who can't spell. This letter is to you and to all those who have given me gifts of education. Gifts I transform and shape and regift to my own students as part of a never-ending chain of educational gifting.

Dear Carl,

Dear All,

Thank You.

References

Bakhtin, M. M. (1986). *Speech genres and other late essays.* Austin, TX: University of Texas Press.

Bakhtin, M. M. (1990). *Art and answerability: Early philosophical essays by M. M. Bakhtin.* Austin, TX: University of Austin Press.

Belliveau, G. (2018). Performing research: Contemplating what it means to be a "man". *Artizein: Arts and Teaching Journal,* 3(1), 38–45.

Fels, L. (2012). Collecting data through performative inquiry: A tug on the sleeve. *Youth Theatre Journal,* 26(1), 50–60. https://doi.org/10.1080/08929092.2012.678209

Fenske, M. (2004). The aesthetic of the unfinished: Ethics and performance. *Text & Performance Quarterly,* 24(1), 1–19. https://doi.org/10.1080/1046293042000239447

Goodall Jr., H. L. (2006). *A need to know: The clandestine history of a CIA family.* Walnut Creek, CA: Left Coast Press.

Holquist, M. (2002). *Dialogism: Bakhtin and his world* (2nd ed.). New York, NY: Routledge.

Irwin, R. L. (2013). Becoming a/r/tography. *Studies in Art Education,* 54(3), 198–215. https://doi.org/10.1080/00393541.2013.11518894

Lea, G. W. (2013). *Homa Bay memories: Using research-based theatre to explore a narrative inheritance* [Doctoral dissertation, The University of British Columbia]. cIRcle. http://circle.ubc.ca/handle/2429/45608

Leggo, C. (2017). The vocation of poetry: Writing a lively love of the world. In L. Butler-Kisber, J. J. Guiney Yallop, M. Stewart, & S. Wiebe (Eds.), *Poetic inquiries of reflection and renewal* (pp. 276–297). Lunenburg, Canada: MacIntyre Purcell.

12 Love in the Time of Covid-19

Contemplating the Gifts, Grace and Gratitude of Carl Leggo as Living with Intellectual Passion

Anita Sinner

The opportunity to participate in this project came during isolation when our world paused collectively and we learned to live a profoundly historic moment suspended with uncertainty. Lingering in liminality, the proposition to express deep appreciation, and sincere thanks to a host of curriculum scholars, both mentors and students, near and far, then and now, evoked an immediate desire to contemplate how we come to love those who gift us with the grace of intellectual passion, and how living with gratitude may be our ultimate reset as educators for a post-pandemic future we could never imagine.

Such a project is inspired and inspiring, and something long overdue in the field. It is far too rare to make spaces amidst our academic responsibilities to properly acknowledge and express our indebtedness to those who guide our living curriculum. If in doubt, take a moment to search your shelves for the number of academic books that include in the index keywords of gifts, grace and gratitude, or legacies for that matter.

And so I begin with a salute to John, a co-editor on this project, who some years ago sent letters of appreciation. How surprised I was to receive a note, and how much it meant to me, and to John, I extend a heartfelt thank you. I treasure your beautifully composed, handwritten words, and always will. Yours is one of the few keepsakes I hold as precious from what has become a lifetime of learning and teaching. For such an act of kindness is precisely what makes a great gift, a moment of grace, and I am most grateful.

As a student-scholar, the cycle of becoming other in the course of academic privilege is one that I have long believed resides in our networks of relations. And when those in our immediate realm come into our lives it is for a reason. So we oscillate in and out of each other's worlds, and often only in hindsight do we realize the scope of contributions and purpose. Some mentors and students stay for a lifetime. Some only briefly. Learning legacies are certainly about the genealogy of thought, but also the integrity of the working relationships we form, and the resonances in our expressions of research that follow. At the same time I wonder: Do we need to also acknowledge the contrary, the truisms of

DOI: 10.4324/9781003154112-13

106 *Anita Sinner*

taking, omissions, or lack of gratitude? Without absence, is it possible to embrace the intensities held in gifts, grace and gratitude? And, how do we embody the qualities of these words, when paying it forward?

Perhaps this tensionality is a requisite trait for intellectual love and passion, timeless and boundless. Perhaps we are the curriculum when we feel both: joy and sorrow, faith and despair, devotion and betrayal. All part of the humanity that can be lost on our academic travels. We must trust the process, for there are only possibilities of choice. It is with mindfulness we may then step back and ask, "What good are we if we disrupt?" When we elect to "stay with the trouble," in a nod to Haraway (2016), it is always contingent on the event, and the desire of the actors.

Contemplating these notions, I soon came to realize that attending to learning legacies was also an impossible task, for the genealogies of ideas require extensive mapping of all the relations that inform, across disciplines and eras, to ensure credit is due. It may be that we are rather more curators of ideas as educators, joining conversations that are already underway and offering our perspectives in intellectual exchanges that are pedagogically collective. So I fear omitting all those dear to me, or naming those who have chosen to live by *dissing*, for they may prove important to learning legacies also. Despite quarantine and academic hearsay, I am still drawn to the light, as is the optimism of a teacher's life. So, in this short rumination, I turn to the acts and actions of one, to consider Carl's influence, to reflect on how his thinking touched so many and built scholarly lives for countless others. I draw in part on the commentary for a book of his collected works, which was a collaboration with Carl and our long-time circle of dear friends, and on my comments prepared for the *Canadian Association of Curriculum Studies* pre-conference to honour Carl, shortly after his passing in 2019. I pause again, as I re-write these words, and remember with gladness our shared scholarly adventures. Carl's contributions to the field became an invitation to countless scholars and students to be part of an academic family where a kinship of ideas and spirit offered a sense of belonging, something I never imagined would be, and something I feel so very fortunate to have experienced in curriculum studies. For me, such a life force as Carl's was and is the essence of learning legacies.

In this unfolding ode to Carl, my venerable advisor, who always guided despite my many missteps over the years: "How do I adore thee? Let me count the ways." Happenstance brought us together nearly two decades ago, during a formative moment in curriculum studies, as the arts became research in a story that is uniquely Canadian. As part of a team, Carl created openings for voices beyond his own, a gift the Oxford dictionary defines as the "voluntary transference without anything in return" (Brown, 1993, p. 1088). In doing so Carl, you set in motion movements to a horizon that I did not know could exist academically. From his lessons, I try to impart the same to my students as best I can,

Love in the Time of Covid-19   107

though I have yet to master these efforts. I know that no matter what I proposed, something daring or something that might be a bit scholarly risqué (see McLaren et al., 2018), Carl was always a willing partner, with the courage to never be afraid to say it like it was, rather than say it for the politics of space. This kind of mentorship is without question "a mode of behavior [or] attitude, adopted with [a] view to elegance [and] refinement" (Brown, 1993, p. 1124), a way of being in the world that models the best in academic character, talent, and ethics, with a standard of personal integrity that encourages others to follow their yearnings, despite hegemonic institutional practices, and those who embody them, and who work so hard to nullify genuine desire.

If I may indulge further to share the "condition of being thankful, with the appreciation and inclination to return kindness" (Brown, 1993, p. 1134), may I say, Carl, your spirit is with us, and much like your longing for more *Picnics*, we want for more intimate conversation with you, where we are "just talking" (Irwin, Hasebe-Ludt & Sinner, 2019, p. 172). Your gracious capacity to make every person feel they were special and that their ideas needed to be heard remain among your greatest gifts.

How do we begin to take up all that is offered of such a rich writerly life, a scholarly life, a spiritual life, a life lived with such generosity? (Irwin, Hasebe-Ludt & Sinner, 2019, p. 175). The humorous sophistication of your poetic propositions always brings us to stories. Your candid and compassionate insights, and appreciation of the irony of the human condition, make us feel, as the backbone of your pedagogic intent, much as you wrote in 1999, we "listen to the light that pulses between the beats in [your] heart" (Irwin, Hasebe-Ludt & Sinner, 2019, p. 188). Perhaps it is in the pleasure we shared, when you told us about your expansive cast of characters and host of plots, with an orator's presence, your gleaming eyes and beautiful flowing hair. Your stories soar in our imagination, like Skipper and his kernels of wisdom (p. 176). Here we find solace. And we walk with you among the chocolate lilies and the laughter of ducks, and follow the teachings of Mr. Burns, and the adventures at Costco, while seizing the moment of your whimsy in a frenzied search for your journal stolen at the beach. Oh what might those pages hold! Yes, you always listened to the light, to tell us stories of matter-ing, of growing up perpendicular on the side of a hill on Lynch's Lane. Your story is a story of a lined life (p. 176).

In 1995, you wrote, "none of my teachers ever encouraged or even suggested that I could write about the ordinary experiences of my daily living" (p. 224). Perhaps this is the legacy we are now charged to fulfil in our scholarly ventures. Much like your performance with Joe Norris (2014) of *What do scholars want?* – one of the most significant arts-based contributions made to education, and a video I share with every class I teach – we must remember to do so with jest, and with appreciation of

108 *Anita Sinner*

our many foibles and follies as scholars. In such exchange we come to know you Carl, the author, through your "word-making," your typology, and your contemplations and speculations, and the finer distinctions of your deliberations with an array of voices that "hold the possibility of generating lively and productive discussion" (see Irwin, Hasebe-Ludt & Sinner, 2019, p. 224).

I remember the first day we met in your office. I noticed your collection of DH Lawrence and I thought, "Ah, a kindred spirit!" Though I must admit, I often wondered about the Tigger collection – an alter-ego perhaps, given your exceptional enthusiasm and always energetic disposition, so full of cheer and optimism and embrace. I smile at this possibility, for the fondness you had in instilling paradoxes of wonder and wonderment, and witticism, within the complex layers of your public persona. To this day, none compare with your idealism, your deep devotion to your faith, your family, your friends, and your steadfast pledge, loyalty, and dependability to your students.

Yes, I will always strive to hold in my heart the moments of Carl.

Carl made storying our lives as teachers and students part of what Gregg and Seigworth (2010) refer to as a growing "social aesthetic," a "public intimacy" that demonstrates the rhythmic art of the everyday as research that is alive and in action. Certainly his defining role in poetic inquiry as theoretical, methodological, and practice in research is without question, and perhaps best encapsulated in his recounting the comments by a reviewer of his masked paper, submitted to a well-respected education journal: "If you knew anything about poetic inquiry, you would have quoted Carl Leggo!" Ah, the irony of academic outrage in yet another Stephen Leacock moment that is imprinted in the logic of the (sometimes dark) humour at the back of everything Carl said with words. Our imagination continues to delight in his ability to communicate his persistent intellectual interest, to convey the human condition with care, acceptance, tolerance, and sensitivity, always showing how education is a form of cultural study, and pedagogy a sensorial experience of love and passion. Badiou (2010) considers love "an essential experience for philosophy," and the vast body of work Carl gifted to curriculum studies, driven by an intense curiosity to know more, has become an ethical encounter, an embrace, a proposition of hope (p. 53).

I have thought a great deal about this notion of legacy because of Carl. Looking back now on *Storying the World*, I notice a remarkable thematic consistency in the titles of his many articles and chapters: Love. Love is the central character of the genealogic project that Carl meticulously documented over decades, in ways Foucault described as requiring "patience and a knowledge of details" for the function of the author to come into being (see Rainbow, 1984, p. 76). Or, to rephrase, this is our inheritance, part of the system of obligation, as Foucault describes,

Love in the Time of Covid-19   109

that we hold in relation to his ideas. Much as Rita expressed, "Carl has continued to be my beacon of light ... guiding me to safety," and that is a sentiment I anticipate many of us share for his storied legacy (Irwin, Hasebe-Ludt & Sinner, 2019, p. 80).

From these brief interludes with Carl we may return to this book project on gifts, grace, and gratitude and take comfort. Having devoted our lives to learning and teaching, and being fortunate enough to join in the complicated world of the academy, honouring the learning legacies of our mentors before us, and our learners after us, seems paramount today as we feel detachments growing, distances harder to bear, and differences in kind lending to division rather than diversity. Yet often in hardship and loss, we can come to live with greater attunement, fidelity, and allegiance. May love guide us.

Cicero (2017/1833) wrote, "There is no duty more indispensable than that of returning a kindness" (p. 27). So to all who share this journey, thank you. You are all learning legacies in your own right, and may we continue to touch our lives together in ways that are deeply felt, and continue to spark the imagination, and may we be grateful for these many gracious gifts. I trust these few words are but a small commentary on the gratitude you all deserve. May the present be guided by your intention, and the future with a purpose that continues to embrace the intellectual passion you awaken. May we follow Carl's wisdom and write ungrammatically, with uneven sentences, and may our stories always end with etcetera.

References

Badiou, A. (2010). *Philosophy and the event.* (L. Burchill, Trans.). Cambridge: Polity.

Brown, L. (Editor-in-Chief). (1993). *The new shorter Oxford English dictionary on historical principles.* New York, NY: Oxford University Press.

Cicero, M. (1833/2017). *Cicero's three books of offices or moral duties.* Miami: HardPress.

Gregg, M., & Seigworth, G. (Eds.). (2010). *The affect theory reader.* Durham: Duke University.

Haraway, D. (2016). *Staying with the trouble: Making kin in the Chthulucene.* Durham: Duke University.

Irwin, R., Hasebe-Ludt, E., & Sinner, A. (2019). *Storying the world: The contributions of Carl Leggo on language and poetry.* New York, NY: Routledge.

McLaren, M., Leggo, C., & Sinner, A. (2018). Wild profusions: An ode to academic hair. *Journal of the Canadian Association of Curriculum Studies: Special Issue, 16, 1.* Available at: https://jcacs.journals.yorku.ca/index.php/jcacs/article/view/40366/36366.

Norris, J. (Director). (2014). *Carl Leggo: What do scholars want?* [Video]. Available from https://www.youtube.com/watch?v=OYfPPEDhH5Q.

Rainbow, P. (Ed.). (1984). *The Foucault reader.* New York, NY: Pantheon Books.

13 The Magic Time

Indigenous Influences on Pedagogies Linking the Past with the Future

Jean-Paul Restoule

There is an exercise I do with my teacher education classes (I've also shared it with a graduating class at the University of Toronto in 2017). It's inspired by Jo-ann Archibald's (2008) retelling of Dr. Vince Stogan's teaching of Hands Back Hands Forward. We gather in a circle and lift our left hands palm up and our right hands palm down. We then join hands with the people standing next to us so that we form a circle. Our left hands are facing up towards the ancestors, our grandmothers, and grandfathers, and bringing down that knowledge from the past, while our right hands reach back to pull forward the beings yet to come, our grandchildren. We represent seven generations when we do this and we connect the past with the future in the present moment. We bring gratitude to what we learned that day and we release all our heaviness, the emotional toll of whatever we encountered and leave in a positive frame. The present is a magical time because it is made possible by what those ancestors did. They made a path for us. If accessing knowledge and being present where we are is something we are able to do it's because they made the conditions possible for that to happen. At the same time, we have to be mindful of what path we are laying for those ones yet to come to follow in our footsteps. This moment is filled with so much potential. So much inheritance. So much responsibility. I find it to be a moment that is both humbling and empowering.

I'd like to take this opportunity provided by the editors of this volume to look with gratitude upon some of the teachers who influenced my ways of teaching, some of them unexpected or unlikely, but nevertheless influential. I would also like to look with hope and purpose to the future by examining what kinds of legacies I am trying to instil with purpose in the present that I hope will carry on in the teachers I hope to inspire by my approaches. In a way this chapter is me trying to recreate that same "magic time" when the present is activated with intention by honouring the past and looking to the future and knowing that where we stand and what we choose to do now, in this moment, is a collection of all the moments that came before and sets in motion all the moments that will follow. Magic.

DOI: 10.4324/9781003154112-14

The Magic Time 111

I have had many teachers that inspired me with some aspect of their approach, their curriculum choices, their words, and their being. Their teachings. Some of the ones who immediately came to mind were Laara Fitznor, Eileen Antone, Grafton Antone, Marlene Cuthbert, Alex McKay, Keren Rice, Deb McGregor, and Ed Doolittle. And as I thought a little longer, some more came to mind: Dorothy Smith, Margrit Eichler, my Windsor Communication Studies profs like Stan Cunningham, Jim Linton, Kai Hildebrandt, Richard Lewis, Irv Goldman, and Kwasi Ansu-Kyeremeh but also my University of Windsor philosophy teachers, Linda Fisher, Kate Parr, Anthony Blair, and Ralph Johnson. Not directly taught by them but influential regardless: Paolo Freire, Stuart Hall, Linda Smith, Graham Smith, Marie Battiste, Jo-ann Archibald, Verna Kirkness, Thomas King. And even Kurt Vonnegut. Elders Lillian McGregor and Lillian Pitawanakwat were influential to me and there were many other Elders and teachings along the way too numerous to mention.

In 1998, there was an Elder guiding a session I was invited to on Institutionalized Racism in Higher Education. She told the group some words I continue to share to this day: "Take what you need and leave the rest." Of course this is a teaching about medicine picking, but she advised us in our learning journeys, especially in western institutions to not carry the racism out with us. It's bad medicine. So don't harvest it. Don't put it in your basket for later. Instead take the things that make you better. The tools and skills you need. The medicine that helps you think more clearly, that helps you be creative. That helps you solve problems. To see in new ways. Take what you need. Leave the rest. I'll be describing some of what I took and I won't mention in this chapter the things I've left aside or behind.

I gathered medicine from Dr. Laara Fitznor. She taught me about using circle, which I have written about elsewhere (Restoule, 2009, 2006). About humour. About giving. And about *kimooci-*, but more on that later.

From Eileen and Grafton Antone I learned about patience and how to help our people. I learned about family and I learned about gentleness and commitment. Importantly, I learned that sometimes, the best way to deliver difficult news or to request or demand something, is with a smile. Grafton taught me that. And he reminded me that many Indigenous people learn cultural traditions, languages, and teachings in the city – not just in First Nations communities. Eileen taught me how far we can go to support students. She even used to phone students to wake them up and remind them to go to class. She waited three years to tell me that I was making a mistake in my identity lectures for Intro to Aboriginal Studies...she gave me the benefit of a doubt once, the chance to correct my mistake a second time and on the third time told me that there were others in the community who would disagree with some of my

112   *Jean-Paul Restoule*

statements. That was a great deal of patience and multiple chances. I still try to assume the best of people in my teaching today.

Keren Rice taught me that everyone has a place and a role to play. Her way of including people and seeing people's strengths has been very important to me. Alex McKay was trusted to deliver many courses in Indigenous Studies and as I learned Anishinaabemowin and Ojibwe culture from him, I learned the power of *kimooci-*. But more on that later.

Deb McGregor gave me my first teaching gig. We met in Laara's course. We worked on an Indigenous knowledge project together. When she and Ed Doolittle co-taught the Intro to Aboriginal Studies course, I was a teaching assistant and on occasion sat in on their lectures. I had so much reverence for their different styles. The tortoise and the hare. Ed would take a long time to think through an answer to a student inquiry and respond with carefully chosen words, taking the time to ensure things were said just right. Deb would drop a flow of many thoughts, many facts, many asides, all brilliant, but at a pace that would leave students breathless just listening. I did not envy notetakers in the second half of that course. But what I learned from her in that first year was the significance of careful course design. It was an intro course and she asked, "What concepts can you absolutely NOT leave this course without knowing?" and then proceeded to fill in the course with those concepts. "You can't graduate from Intro to ABS without knowing the meaning of title, treaty, co-existence, Guswentha, Indian Act, residential schools, and so on." When planning my courses today, I still think about what it is I want the students to leave knowing. For instance, when planning our MOOC in 2012, the design team and I chose the topics by thinking what concepts MUST be addressed? We were also guided by Verna Kirkness and Ray Barnhardt's (1991) article on the 4R's of Higher Education.

I first read Freire (1970; 1973) in one of Marlene Cuthbert's courses. She was my Master of Arts supervisor and in her courses, I liked how she talked about the state of global relations with simple language and little jargon and such force and clarity. She was an embodiment of Freirean communication. I took from Freire the concept of praxis, of theory informing action informing theory informing action and constantly in motion. A process. It jibed well with Indigenous teachings I was learning at that same time in my life too. I found it appealing to situate learning in the everyday with the notion that change for social justice is the aim. I valued the action-oriented approach. I wanted people to learn in ways that just didn't become rote facts or repeating things back to me but that transformed who they were and what they did. The best compliment I could receive in my education work was to hear that after my course, a learner changed how they saw things or who they were and tried to make their self, their family, their community, their school, their classroom, their workplace a little different. More Indigenous, maybe. Not

The Magic Time   113

appropriate, but informed by Indigenous knowing, Indigenous being, Indigenous ethics.

To me, these gifts are very much tools for living well in the present. George Dei (2000) taught that tradition is what we learn from the past that enables us to live well in the present. I feel that Indigenous knowledge is very much needed for all of us to live well in the present and I teach in such a way that I hope my students take this notion away. Even if much of its wisdom has a continuity with the past, Indigenous knowledge is meant to be engaged in present times.

From Blair and Johnson (1993) I picked up Logical Self-Defence: the skills to identify fallacious reasoning and how to build a stronger argument. Thanks Tony and Ralph. I try to help graduate students with their arguments, ensuring they don't make fallacious mistakes in their reasoning. Speaking of helping graduate students, one of the most helpful techniques in my student days was meeting in a thesis group, sharing our work, and progress in circle. I learned this from my doctoral supervisor, Margrit Eichler, and instituted it with my students at the Ontario Institute for Studies in Education. The thesis group allowed for a cohort to learn from one another, for those further along to share tips and model that there is an end in sight, for students to share resources, struggles, and gains. This approach was largely evident in SAGE or Supporting Aboriginal Graduate Enhancement (Pidgeon, Archibald, & Hawkey, 2014). I was inspired by the work Jo-ann Archibald was doing in British Columbia with grad students and encouraged colleagues and friends to take up the approach in Ontario.

It's important to note that SAGE was informed by the Maori and Indigenous (MAI) programme in Aotearoa, and Graham Smith brought the approach to BC during his time at the University of British Columbia. Besides SAGE, one of the biggest influences Graham had on me was the approach of centring Indigenous perspectives, worldviews, and knowledges. While many of the scholars I was reading were taking an anti-colonial approach, both Laara and Graham centred their own peoples' knowledge and started with their own teachings, wisdom, and traditions. While doing so still bumps up against the colonizer inevitably, it's not the main focus. The agenda is set differently this way. Instead of reacting to what the colonizer is doing, you can begin from affirming, positive, life-sustaining, Indigenous approaches (Smith, 1998). This was a great gift that has influenced my research, my teaching, and my life. I find in my classrooms today, when we begin from an Indigenous way, it just makes everything flow better. It allows me to model Indigenous worldviews, perspectives, knowledges, and pedagogies so that it is experienced and learned holistically; we're doing it and not just talking about it.

One of the things that happens when we centre Anishinaabe ways of learning is that we inevitably "kimooc" things at some point. Kimooci-is a modifier in the Ojibwe language that when added to a verb, describes

114   *Jean-Paul Restoule*

that the action is being done in a sneaky way. You might achieve one goal by coming at it in a covert way. This word has been incredibly descriptive and tactical in my academic life and allows me to survive and make things happen that might not have been possible if everything were done out in the open. It's a lot of fun too. When my classes are in on the kimooc we all have a great laugh.

Laughs and wisdom combined is something I pulled out of Kurt Vonnegut's writing, an author I've enjoyed since I was in high school and whom I now see influencing the way I see the world. Themes running through his work are the importance of being kind ("Goddammit you got to be..."), being present in life's sweet moments ("If this isn't great, I don't know what is"), being yourself (from the particular emerges the universal), and finding hope and goodness when surrounded by the evils of boundless corporatism, excessive (any) militarism, vacuous cultural norms, hypocrisy, vanity, social inequities, and so on. While I have a cynical view of the world we live in, I also believe we must be kind to one another, and that there is goodness in our fellow humans. We are all unwavering bands of light, no better than any other life form, and ensuring we can all be the best we can be, and use our talents to help others, then we will leave the world a better place than we found it.

I have had many students who have pushed my learning and teaching. I think of the ones who made me take a second look at my resources or readings, either critically or in one case, to see the positives in a work I thought was seriously limited. I've been challenged to provide deeper and more difficult Indigenous engagement. When I've struggled with my own sense of authenticity to teach this material, I was introduced to the concept of the imposter syndrome by one of my students. This concept has been very useful in counselling others who are the first in their family to attend university, to hold certain leadership positions, and to feel that they are entitled to the place they find themselves in. I've also been inspired by students to change the writing assignments I used for assessment. I watched colleagues design Indigenous courses where the assignment is weaving, beading, sewing, or some other artistic project. It made me realize the irony of teaching Indigenous topics but requiring only written assignments. Over time I've tried to make it possible to have courses where at least 50% of the grade, and potentially much more (up to student choice), can be non-written, creative projects. This is an attempt to better embody and represent Indigenous worldviews and knowledges.

I am hopeful when I see teachers embrace their responsibilities; try new things; learn from their mistakes; dive in, but critically reflect on what they're doing; who challenge themselves by learning in the spaces of discomfort; who bring their vulnerabilities to class and their creativity to the fore. I am hopeful for a more just future, a decolonial future, a relational future, a future of language, culture and values,

The Magic Time 115

a future of healthy vibrant ecosystems, where ceremony connects us to one another and to the land and to community. Those mentioned here provided good medicine that I took with me and try to share with others in my teaching.

References

Archibald, J. (Q'um Q'um Xiiem). (2008). *Indigenous storywork principles: Educating the heart, mind, body, and spirit.* Vancouver: UBC Press.

Dei, G. (2000). African development: The relevance and implications of 'Indigenousness'. In Dei, G, Hall, B., & Rosenberg, D. G. *Indigenous knowledge in global contexts: Multiple readings of our world, pp. 70–86.* Toronto: OISE/UT Press.

Freire, P. (1970). *Pedagogy of the oppressed.* New York, NY: Continuum.

Freire, P. (1973). *Education for critical consciousness.* New York, NY: Seabury Press.

Johnson, R., & Blair, J. A. (1993). *Logical self-defence, 3rd Ed.* Toronto: McGraw-Hill Ryerson.

Kirkness, V., & Barnhardt, R. (1991). First nations and higher education: The four R's-respect, relevance, reciprocity, responsibility. *Journal of American Indian Education, 30*(3), 1–16.

Pidgeon, M., Archibald, J., & Hawkey, C. (2014). Relationships matter: Supporting Aboriginal graduate students in British Columbia Canada. *Canadian Journal of Higher Education, 44*(1), 1–21.

Restoule, J. P. (2006). *Learning about male Aboriginal identity formation in Toronto using Circle Methodology.* Proceedings of the annual conference, Canadian Association for the Study of Adult Education, (CASAE), pp. 185–190, 2006.

Restoule, J. P. (2009). *Circle methodology and male Aboriginal identity formation.* Within and Beyond Borders: Critical Multicultural Counselling in Practice (Critical Multicultural Counselling Series), Oulanova, O.; Stein, I.; Rai, A.; Hammer, M.; & Poulin, P. (Eds.). Centre for Diversity in Counselling and Psychotherapy, OISE/UT, Toronto. Available: (http://www.oise.utoronto.ca/cdcp/UserFiles/File/Publications/within_and_beyond_borders.pdf).

14 A Curriculum Journey Inspired by Picturebooks

Tara-Lynn Scheffel

> *Morris Lessmore loved words.*
> *He loved stories.*
> *He loved books.*
> [Excerpt from *The Fantastic Flying Books of Mr. Morris Lessmore*]

In this picturebook by William Joyce, Morris Lessmore meets a lady "pulled along by a festive squadron of flying books" who leads him to a library-like room filled with "the faint chatter of a thousand different stories...whispering an invitation to adventure." Morris begins a life among the books, trying to keep them organized and finding satisfaction in caring for them. He gets lost in books, shares them with others, and believes "everyone's story matters." The books become old friends to Morris until one day, he flies away on a similar squadron of flying books and the story begins again as a young girl takes his place.

Like Morris Lessmore, I also love stories and books. Stories have carried me away and taken me to new places, and I share them with others. They have also informed my curricular decision-making as a literacy teacher and teacher educator. In this chapter, I reconnect with my lived experiences. What emerges and seeks my attention (Shields, 2005) is the image of my bookshelf (see image 14.1) filled with picturebooks that hold stories of my curricular journey as a learner, literacy educator, and researcher. My bookshelf beckons me to look "inward, outward, backward and forward" (Clandinin & Connelly, 2000, p. 48) to put into words what I have learned from my collection. It is a journey of love and legacy.

Before the Bookshelf: Looking Back

> *Where did this love of reading begin? I recall frequent trips to story-hour at the local library, and that wonderful time before bed cuddling in the blankets listening to a favourite story - Disney Golden Books, Mother Goose, and other fairy tale collections come to mind. I learned to read at school with Dick and Jane and Mr. Mugs but recall shelves of picturebooks for independent reading. The first book*

DOI: 10.4324/9781003154112-15

A Curriculum Journey Inspired by Picturebooks

Image 14.1 "A Close-Up of My Bookshelf" photograph by "Tara-Lynn Scheffel."

I remember from school is one that my grade three teacher read aloud to the class - it told of Pippi Longstocking and from her striped stockings to her horizontal braids, I thought she was wonderful! At home, I read [a legacy of] books passed down from my mother - The Bobbsey Twins and Nancy Drew adventures - and other books like Anne of Green Gables trigger fond reading memories.

Looking back, reading was a positive experience and I suspect my love of reading comes in part from these early feelings of support and success, along with ongoing access to books. I took this positive experience with me as an educator, wanting to emulate what my teachers had done.

A Beginning Bookshelf: Still Looking Back

As a new teacher, I regularly explored the shelves of local bookstores to build my classroom library. Every New Year's Day, I recruited my father to go with me to a clearance sale to load up on new picturebooks for my classroom. I kept a running wish list of picturebooks I heard about at workshops and from other educators. I placed the more expensive hardcover picturebooks on my special teacher shelf behind my desk saving them for a specific teaching/learning moment.

Those picturebooks on my special teacher shelf hold some of my most precious memories from my early teaching days. I loved the rhythm of the stories, the tone and intonation that created suspense or laughter, and invited students' engagement as the story within the pages unfolded. I loved these books and the potential they generated for discussion, storytelling, drama, writing and more. The picturebooks on this shelf served as inspiration for the choral reading events my class would share during chapels and assemblies. Some were integrated into themed units I created for social studies and science, while others were reserved for holidays like Christmas or Easter.

118 *Tara-Lynn Scheffel*

As an educator, I wanted to help my students discover "an immeasurable gift" (Miller, 2012, p. 92) in reading, one that was supported by time spent reading but also the freedom to choose books of interest, that leads to enjoyment and lifelong learning. To allow for this choice, I built a literacy-rich classroom library (Axelrod et al., 2015) with picturebooks a key staple to supplement the more restrictive basal reading series I was teaching with at the time. Looking back, my special bookshelf held the picturebooks with the greatest curricular potential. I offered them to students only after we had read them, moving them to the front ledge of the classroom rather than the classroom library. I remember this struggle as a new educator investing in picturebooks, often from my own funds, but feeling they were worth the investment for my students. The bookshelf that I began teaching with was reflective of the lens established before I knew I was looking (Shields, 2005). It was during graduate school that I became more cognizant of what was on my bookshelf and what was missing.

A Bookshelf Inspired by Experiences: From Then to Now

Graduate school first prompted me to look more critically at the picturebooks on my bookshelf. During a narrative inquiry course, I noticed that while my students and I fell captive to one book's imaginative quest involving friendship, rescue and the occasional funny antic, I had not looked beyond the surface of the story at its generalizations and stereotypes around gender. With this realization, I began to explore underlying messages within the images of children's stories in ways I had not done before.

My bookshelf expanded and changed as I sought out social issue picturebooks and multiple-perspective texts to bridge discussions with learners around issues of power and positioning (Clarke & Whitney, 2009) and different worldviews (Laminack & Kelly, 2019). Dual language picturebooks and picturebooks representing other cultures have also found a home on my bookshelf. It is not that my bookshelf was devoid of such books previously but that I had not considered just how important it was that books offer mirrors and windows where children can see not only themselves but others (Axelrod et al., 2015; Sims Bishop, 1990).

Over time, my bookshelf became entwined with life experiences, such as the alphabet books added to my collection during trips afar or my collection of intergenerational books that began with research experiences (Scheffel, 2015; Scheffel & McKee, 2019). These picturebooks, and others on my shelf, are integral to readings I assign in teacher education courses to bridge the why with the how.

My bookshelf continues to expand. It has grown with the times to include new genres such as graphic novels that were not as

A Curriculum Journey Inspired by Picturebooks 119

prevalent or valued when I first began teaching. As more text formats have become available, it has extended to include a digital shelf on my computer.

As I look at my bookshelf of picturebooks in the present (physical and digital), I find myself reflecting on the ways that "curriculum is all of life's experience" (Shields & Reid-Patton, 2009, p. 6). Portelli and Vibert (2002) describe a "curriculum of life" that involves "a dynamic relationship among teachers, students, knowledge, and contexts" (p. 36). My bookshelf has similarities in the ways it speaks to the curriculum journey of my life as a literacy teacher, teacher educator, and researcher. It is unique to me and my experiences, built one book at a time through the relationships I have formed over time – for which I am forever grateful.

A Bookshelf as Legacy: Looking to the Future

My bookshelf is a legacy passed to me through my early home and school experiences, which has expanded through my experiences as a teacher and learner. I hope to pass this legacy of love for picturebooks to my students. Recently, a teacher candidate, referred to my bookshelf as she reflected on her learning in an early literacy course (used with permission):

> Dear Tara-Lynn,
> This course has made me realize how important it is to have a special bookshelf in your house or office that you can share with your friends and family. The support of family is critical to developing early literacy skills. I am lucky enough to have such a wonderful support system at home… I am proud to say I have started my own special bookshelf in my room and I can't wait to see how much it grows. So once again, thank you for sharing your passion and knowledge on early literacy and further sharing your special bookshelf with me. - Sarah

I was also inspired by other educators. My family gifted me books, as did the families I taught. In this way, gifts and legacy are interconnected. Sarah's words prompt me to think about the legacy of the picturebooks that are central to my pedagogical practices as a teacher educator.

Like De Groot (2007), I share the desire for teacher candidates "to be encouraged to reflect on the importance of using and reading children's literature of all kinds to be prepared to share these books with their future students" (p. 21). Though students, parents, and teachers often abandon picturebooks beyond elementary classrooms, they hold much potential for teaching and learning (Roser, Martinez, & Fowler-Amato,

120   Tara-Lynn Scheffel

2011) and can be used with children of all ages to support comprehension through the inclusion of pictures and written text (Burke & Collier, 2017). Picturebooks with accessible text can be particularly supportive to English language learners (Harvey & Goudvis, 2004). As a teacher educator, I find that picturebooks offer a similar form of accessible text to use in class together as teacher candidates try various literacy teaching/learning strategies. Picturebooks spark dialogue around concepts such as multimodal literacy (Leland, Harste & Huber, 2005; Martens et al., 2012) as well as specific comprehension strategies like questioning (Lohfink, 2012), inferencing (Bintz et al., 2012), speaking and listening strategies (Mills, 2010) and purposeful and meaningful uses of different genres and formats like wordless books (Serafini, 2014); nonfiction (Stead, 2014); dual-language books (Axelrod et al., 2015, p. 21); and multilevel texts (Cornford, 2012).

Though I remain cognizant that my time is limited "to delve into a multitude of books for ongoing conversation" (Scheffel et al., 2018. p. 2), they are part of my legacy. Picturebooks have become a resource for my teaching and a conduit for me to reflect on and learn about my practice (Heydon, Hibbert, & Iannacci, 2004). Some picturebooks on my shelf are borrowed from the library for a short time and returned. Others have with me for a long time – from my early days as a teacher. When I run out of room, parting with a book is made easier by passing it forward to a new teacher.

As I gaze upon my bookshelf, I am grateful for the gifts these picturebooks have had on my teaching and learning, and my own curriculum journey. I am also filled with hope for the ways that (picture)books can offer a bridge to new ideas and alternate views (Laminack & Kelly, 2019), become windows and mirrors through which learners can see themselves and help us to apply critical eyes towards the picturebooks we select to disrupt what Adichi (2009) calls "single stories" (Tschida, Ryan, & Ticknor, 2014).

My legacy as a teacher educator is built on picturebooks, one book at a time. May you find your path as you think about your favourites.

Morris liked to share the books with others. Sometimes it was a favorite that everyone loved, and other times he found a lonely little volume whose tale was seldom told.
[Excerpt from *The Fantastic Flying Books of Mr. Morris Lessmore* by William Joyce]

References

Adichi, C.N. (2009). The Danger of a Single Story by Chimamanda Ngozi Adichie, TEDGlobal: https://www.ted.com/talks/chimamanda_ngozi_adichie_the_danger_of_a_single_story.

A Curriculum Journey Inspired by Picturebooks   121

Axelrod, Y., Hall, A. H., & McNair, J. C. (2015). A is Burrito and B is sloppy Joe: Creating print-rich environments for children in K-3 classrooms. *Young Children, 70*(4), 16–25.

Bintz, W. P., Moran, P., Berndt, R., Ritz, E., Skilton, J. A., & Bircher, L. S. (2012). Using Literature to Teach Inference across the Curriculum. *Voices from the Middle, 20*(1), 16–24.

Burke, A., & Collier, D. (2017). 'I was kind of teaching myself': Teachers' conversations about social justice and teaching for change. *Teacher Development, 21*(2), 268–287.

Clandinin, D. J., & Connelly, F. M. (2000). What do narrative inquirers do? In *Narrative inquiry: Experience and story in qualitative research.* San Francisco, CA: Jossey-Bass.

Clarke, L. W., & Whitney, E. (2009). Walking in their shoes: Using multiple-perspectives texts as a bridge to critical literacy. *The Reading Teacher, 62*(6), 530–534.

Cornford, C. (2012). *Using Multilevel Texts.* What Works? Research into Practice. Literacy and Numeracy Secretariat. http://www.edu.gov.on.ca/eng/literacynumeracy/inspire/research/WW_Multilevel_Texts.pdf.

De Groot, J. (2007). Preservice teachers and children's literature: Implications for teacher-librarians. *Teacher Librarian, 35*(2), 18–22.

Harvey, S., & Goudvis, A. (2004). *Strategic thinking: Reading and responding, grades 4–8.* Portland, ME: Stenhouse Publishers.

Heydon, R., Hibbert, K., & Iannacci, L. (2004). Strategies to support balanced literacy approaches in pre- and inservice teacher education. *Journal of Adolescent & Adult Literacy, 48*(4), 312–319.

Laminack, L. L., & Kelly, K. (2019). *Reading to make a difference: Using literature to help students speak freely, think deeply, and take action.* Portsmouth, NH: Heinemann.

Leland, C. H., Harste, J. C., & Huber, K. R. (2005). Out of the box: Critical literacy in a first-grade classroom. *Language Arts, 82*(4), 257–268.

Lohfink, G. (2012). (2012). Promoting self-questioning through picture book illustrations. *The Reading Teacher, 66*(4), 295–299.

Martens, P., Martens, R., Doyle, M. H., Loomis, J., & Aghalarov, S. (2012). Learning from picturebooks: Reading and writing multimodally in first grade. *The Reading Teacher, 66*(4), 285–294.

Miller, D. (2012). Creating a classroom where readers flourish. *The Reading Teacher, 66*(2), 88–92.

Mills, K. A. (2010). Floating on a sea of talk: Reading comprehension through speaking and listening. *The Reading Teacher, 63*(4), 325–329.

Portelli, J. P., & Vibert, A. B. (2002). A curriculum of life. *Education Canada, 42*, 36–39.

Roser, N., Martinez, M., & Fowler-Amato, M. (2011). The power of picturebooks. *Voices from the Middle, 19*(1), 24–31.

Scheffel, T. (2015). The heart of the matter: Exploring intergenerational themes in children's literature. *Journal of Intergenerational Relationships, 13*(2), 167–181.

Scheffel, T., Cameron, C., Dolmage, L., Johnston, M., Lapensee, J., Solymar, K., Usher-Speedie, E., & Wills, M. (2018). The journey of a collaborative children's literature book club for teacher candidates. *Reading Horizons, 57*(1), 1–14.

122 *Tara-Lynn Scheffel*

Scheffel, T., & McKee, L. (2019). Uniting generations: Intergenerational and universal-themed picturebook recommendations. *Journal of Childhood Studies*, *44*(5), 120–128. doi: https://doi.org/10.18357/jcs00019339.

Serafini, F. (2014). Exploring wordless picturebooks. *The Reading Teacher*, *68*(1), 24–26.

Shields, C. (2005). Using narrative inquiry to inform and guide our (RE) interpretations of lived experience. *McGill Journal of Education (MJE)*, *40*(1), 179–188.

Shields, C., & Reid-Patton, V. (2009). A curriculum of kindness: (Re) creating and nurturing heart and mind through teaching and learning. *Brock Education*, *18*(2), 4–15.

Sims Bishop, R. (1990). Mirrors, windows, and sliding glass doors. *Perspectives*, *6*(3), ix–xi.

Stead, T. (2014). Nurturing the inquiring mind through the nonfiction read-aloud. *The Reading Teacher*, *67*(7), 488–495.

Tschida, C. M., Ryan, C. L., & Ticknor, A. S. (2014). Building on windows and mirrors: Encouraging disruption of 'single stories' through children's literature. *Journal of Children's Literature*, *40*(1), 28–39.

15 (Re)membering Indigenous Curriculum Theorists
Gifts and Gratitude

Adrian M. Downey

Working against Replacement

In the first curriculum studies course of my master's degree, the instructor said there were no Indigenous curriculum theorists. Their criterion for considering a scholar a curriculum theorist was self-identification and, to a certain degree, that instructor was correct. There are not many Indigenous scholars who call themselves curriculum theorists, nor are there as many who write in the field of curriculum as there could be. This absence is systemic and part of a ubiquitous phenomenon in scholarship broadly and curriculum studies specifically: the erasure of Indigenous intellectual contributions. In a 2013 article in *The Journal of Curriculum Theorizing*, Tuck and Gaztambide-Fernández name this phenomenon as replacement, where marginalized scholars, teachers, and curriculum theorists are intellectually and physically displaced in favour of settlers who reiterate the same ideas in less overtly controversial and/or more academically palatable ways. In this, settler colonialism, as structurally manifest in the scholarly community, has facilitated a historical absence of Indigenous scholars from the field of curriculum studies (see also Sabzalian, 2018; Tuck, 2011).

Tuck and Gaztambide-Fernández's (2013) response to replacement is to divest from the field of curriculum studies, carving their own space (rematriation; see also Tuck, 2011) that "does not try to rescue curriculum studies from its own problematic tendencies" (p. 85). This is an act of refusal on their part, a way of saying "no" to the coopting of Indigenous knowledges by whitestream curriculum scholarship. This refusal may explain why few Indigenous folks who write about the core concerns of curriculum identify with the field, and perhaps why those who might be considered Indigenous curriculum theorists often opt for less ostentatious titles. There are some things academia ought not to claim, and my intent here is not to claim these scholars for the field of curriculum studies. Rather, this chapter seeks to work against this history of replacement and erasure by (re)membering the many Indigenous scholars who have engaged curricular concerns through their work. I model my use

DOI: 10.4324/9781003154112-16

124   *Adrian M. Downey*

of the term (re)membering after Kanyen'keha:ka scholar Sandra Styres (2017), who notes the parenthetical use of *re-* is "visually and linguistically aligned with the concept of circularity" (p. 4) and that the use of *-ing* indicates "fluidity, movement, and progressive action" (p. 4). Here, (re)membering is a personal undertaking rooted in a desire to raise up the work of Indigenous scholars who have informed my thinking and practice. (Re)membering, thorough the evocation of memory, frames the scope of this chapter. This essay is non-exhaustive, and the names I raise up here are those who have been most influential to me as an emerging Indigenous curriculum theorist (I am Mi'kmaq with family ties in the Qalipu Mi'kmaq First Nation. I also have Irish settler ancestry on my father's side). These are scholars I (re)visit often and (re)member actively. I conclude this chapter by offering words of gratitude for the insights they have shared.

(Re)membering

Curriculum theory is often concerned with determining what knowledge is of most worth and what stories are worth telling (Donald, 2016). For too long the answer was White, Eurocentric knowledge and mythology, to the exclusion of all else. Whether named as curriculum theory or not, many Indigenous scholars have critiqued this eurocentrism and engaged the core concerns named above. Battiste (Mi'kmaq) and Henderson's (Chickasaw/Cheyenne) 2000 (Battiste & Henderson, 2000) book, *Protecting Indigenous Knowledge and Heritage,* for example, marks an early articulation of the tenor of Indigenous knowledges and a sustained defence of their validity in relation to dominant Western ways of knowing – a critique Battiste later contextualized in education through *Decolonizing Education* (Battiste, 2013). Battiste's more recent works on treaty (Battiste, 2016a) and Mi'kmaw humanities (Battiste, 2016b) continue engaging Indigenous knowledge in education and beyond. These more recent texts have in some ways contributed foundational understandings to the current curricular movement towards treaty education in Nova Scotia, which encourages all stakeholders in education to understand the relationships established in the Peace and Friendship Treaties.

Over the course of her career, Battiste has offered both critical defences of decolonization, Indigenous sovereignty, and anti-racist education and grounded articulations of Indigenous knowledges and cultural tradition (particularly literacy). *Decolonizing Education* (2013) was a blending of these interconnected facets of contemporary Indigenous thought and showcased the way traditional knowledges and culture can form a precise and expansive response to settler colonialism and its attempted erasure of Indigenous bodies. Likewise, Fyre Jean Graveline's (Métis/Cree) 1998 *Circle Works* is an underappreciated classic in terms of its visioning of a

(Re)membering Indigenous Curriculum Theorists 125

combination between the critical pedagogies of the Marxist tradition and Indigenous thinking, teaching, and learning. In this, Graveline's work is something akin to an Indigenous critical pedagogy – a label that could also apply to Sandy Grande's (Quechua) ground-breaking *Red Pedagogy* (Grande, 2015), which brought the literature of critical pedagogy into conversation with the socio-political context of Indigenous life (particularly in the United States). Unangax̂ scholar Eve Tuck (2011), who sometimes writes in the area of curriculum, but whose work extends well beyond it as well, is likewise concerned with disrupting and speaking back to the curricular manifestations of settler colonialism. Her aforementioned article with Gaztambide-Fernández (2013) also explicitly calls to task the white male settler "founders" of the field, specifically Bobbit, Mann, and Dewey, proposing a shift in our attention away from these folks towards those marginalized voices that have been historically excluded from the complicated conversation.

Another foundational thinker in Indigenous education who could (and ought to) be more widely considered by those in the field of curriculum theory is Gregory Cajete (Tewa). His (Cajete, 1994) 1994 book *Look to the Mountain* is replete with spiritual, cultural, and practical lessons learned from the study of education within an Indigenous worldview. For Cajete, the purpose of education is to find face and find heart – what some have described as discerning who we are, where we come from, why we are here, and where we are going (Downey, 2020). This educative quest for purpose reframes the central curricular question of what knowledge is of most worth towards understandings of self in much the same manner as the reconceptualists. Yet, Cajete's meaning is a self-understanding mobilized outward, into a deep spirit of relationality with other living beings. In this way, Cajete's call for a curriculum of self-knowledge – an educational focus on finding personal purpose and meaning – might more accurately be considered knowledge of self-in-relation (see Graveline 1998; Styres, 2017). In that, Cajete's thinking feels particularly relevant in today's intellectual climate where posthumanism and so-called "new" materialisms invite a more interconnected worldview (see also Todd, 2016).

Self-in-relation is a manifestation of relationality, and pervasive relationality – an interconnectedness with all living beings – is foundational to many Indigenous knowledges. One expression of this relationality unique to the Canadian landscape of curriculum studies is métissage, or the blending together of divergent stories, experiences, thoughts, and ideas through a collective life writing. Dwayne Donald (Cree), who labels himself "an apprentice to curriculum" (Donald, 2016, p. 12), has articulated métissage as an Indigenous approach to research (Donald, 2012) and a curricular process that can displace what he calls the colonial logic of the frontier manifest in the fort (Donald, 2009) – a spatial and onto-epistemic separation of settler and Indigenous worlds.

126 *Adrian M. Downey*

Anishinaabe/Métis scholar Vicki Kelly (2010, 2020) also frequently uses métissage in her work. She takes an artistic approach to her theorizing, bringing life writing, visual arts, and music together towards evocative, provocative, and grounded expressions of lived Indigenous knowledge and, more recently, Indigenous poesies (Kelly, 2019, 2020). The rich, artistic theorizing offered by Kelly is a unique contribution and draws together so many of the divergent threads of Canadian curriculum studies – the arts, spirituality, ecology, social justice, and learning.

Métissage conceptually functions as a tangible approach to truth and reconciliation through the holding together of divergent experiences within our shared places. The meeting grounds between Indigenous and non-Indigenous people can be tense, and they are never absent of the socio-historical power structures endemic to the fabric of society – particularly settler colonialism, patriarchy, and racism (Brayboy, 2005). Yet, meeting, conversing, and learning together are necessities not just of modern schooling and education more broadly, but also of moving towards truth and reconciliation as a society. Willie Ermine's (Cree) foundational notion of ethical space offers a way forward in its articulation of reciprocal and relational contact between Indigenous and settler people(s). Indeed, where the colonial logic has been one of both epistemic and material separation, Indigenous worldviews are often founded on relationship. Donald's (2009, 2016) notion of ethical relationality expands ethical space beyond the dualism of settler-Indigenous relations to include the more-than-humans with which we are always co-present: "Ethical relationality is an ecological understanding of organic connectivity that becomes readily apparent to us as human beings when we honour the sacred ecology that supports all life and living" (Donald, 2016, p. 11). Our curricular encounters, then, are never just between ourselves and the other, but also inhabited by the presence, power, and personality of place – the living Land.

Many contemporary Indigenous scholars have devoted considerable attention to ethical space and ethical relationality. In her master's thesis (Brant-Birioukov, 2017) Kiera Brant-Birioukov (Haudenosaunee), for example, focused on the relationship between settler teacher candidates and Indigenous knowledge as represented in the current movement towards reconciliation. This localization of ethical space and ethical relationality in the context of teacher education offers hope that the next generation of students taught by these teachers-to-be will walk away from their mandatory schooling with a deeper understanding of the implicit relationship between Indigenous and settler folk. In a recent podcast (Ng-A-Fook & Brant-Birioukov, 2020), Brant-Birioukov offered further insight into the complexities at play in working with settler teacher-candidates through the notion of ethical space. As I understood her, ethical space is not the same as safe space; ethical space is relational in its orientation, meaning that safety is understood within the context of the specific relationships of the people (and others) within

(Re)membering Indigenous Curriculum Theorists 127

a space. This is a significant distinction in working with settler teacher candidates as it enables the opportunity to encounter knowledges that may be uncomfortable while still maintaining an ethical frame. Space, as has been well noted, can never be assured of its safety – specifically in this context for Indigenous folk teaching about topics with which they have an intimate lived history. Here, I think of Daniel Heath Justice (Cherokee) – another Indigenous scholar who certainly warrants further consideration in curriculum studies. Justice (2018) reminds us that raising one another up and holding one another to account are not mutually exclusive but, rather, extensions of a strong relationship. In an ethical space, then, we may not excuse those with whom we are in relation from the ethical imperative of confronting their biases and reframing their understandings of the myths foundational to their worldviews.

Words of Gratitude

My goal here has been to disrupt the notion that there are no Indigenous curriculum theorists – however complicated and contested a term that might be. While my tone has been academic in my attempt to offer an accounting of some key Indigenous engagements the core concerns of curriculum, the scope of this chapter has been intimately personal. The scholars whose work I have discussed here have touched my mind and stayed with me in my heart. They are the names that appear over and over again in my work and whose thoughts haunt my own even when unnamed. There are, of course, many non-Indigenous scholars who fall into this category as well – Ted Aoki, Cynthia Chambers, Madeline Grumet, Ashwani Kumar, Carl Leggo, and William Pinar to name a few – but the Indigenous scholars discussed above have a special place in my thinking, unique in our sharing of the bizarre experience of being Indigenous in the academy. In that, we walk in two worlds, speak two languages, and see with two eyes. In graduate school, we learn words like epistemology and learn to critique notions like "best-practices," while along our own journeys we learn the words of our heart, the words of the land – words that in Mi'kmaw sounds like *etuaptmumk* (two-eyed seeing) and *netukulimk* (sustainability). Learning to pronounce those words and etching their meaning into the core of my being has been as much a part of my lived curriculum as reading articles, attending conferences, and writing my dissertation. And I hear those experiences and teachings echoed in the Indigenous scholars above. It is with all sincerity that I extend my gratitude to those above and to those who I have missed. Wela'lioq, thank you all for your words that sit in my heart and in my mind. I will do my best to carry forward your teachings in a good way.

M'sit No'kmaw.
All my relations.

128   Adrian M. Downey

References

Battiste, M. (2013). *Decolonizing education: Nourishing the learning spirit.* Saskatoon: Purich.

Battiste, M. (Ed.). (2016a). *Living treaties: Narrating Mi'kmaw treaty relations.* Sydney, Nova Scotia: Cape Breton University Press.

Battiste, M. (Ed.). (2016b). *Visioning a Mi'kmaw humanities: Indigenizing the academy.* Sydney, Nova Scotia: Cape Breton University Press.

Battiste, M. A., & Henderson, J. Y. (2000). *Protecting Indigenous knowledge and heritage: A global challenge.* Saskatoon: Purich.

Brant-Birioukov, K. (2017). *'But how does this help me?':(Re)thinking (re)conciliation in teacher education* (Master's thesis). Ottawa, ON: University of Ottawa.

Brayboy, B. M. J. (2005). Toward a tribal critical race theory in education. *Urban Review: Issues and Ideas in Public Education, 37*(5), 425–446.

Cajete, G. (1994). *Look to the mountain: An ecology of indigenous education.* Durango, CO: Kivakí Press.

Donald, D. (2009). Forts, curriculum, and Indigenous Métissage: Imagining decolonization of Aboriginal-Canadian relations in educational contexts. *First Nations Perspectives, 2*(1), 1–24.

Donald, D. (2012). Indigenous Métissage: A decolonizing research sensibility. *International Journal of Qualitative Studies in Education, 25*(5), 533–555.

Donald, D. (2016). From what does ethical relationality flow? An "Indian" act in three artifacts. In J. Seidel & D.W. Jardine (Eds.), *The Ecological Heart of Teaching: Radical Tales of Refuge and Renewal for Classrooms and Communities* (pp. 10–16). New York, NY: Peter Lang.

Downey, A. (2020). A reflection on white-seeming privilege through the process of currere. *The Currere Exchange Journal, 3*(2), 1–10.

Grande, S. (2015). *Red pedagogy: Native American social and political thought.* Lanham, MD: Rowman & Littlefield.

Graveline, F. (1998). *Circle works: Transforming eurocentric consciousness.* Halifax, NS: Fernwood.

Justice, D. (2018). *Why Indigenous literatures matter.* Waterloo, Ontario, Canada: Wilfrid Laurier University Press.

Kelly, V. (2010). Finding face, finding heart, and finding foundation: Life writing and the transformation of educational practice. *Transnational Curriculum Inquiry, 7*(2), 82–100.

Kelly, V. (2019). Indigenous poiesis: Medicine for Mother Earth. *Artizein: Arts and Teaching Journal, 4*(1), 17–30.

Kelly, V. (2020). Living and being in place: An Indigenous métissage. In E. Lyle (Ed.), *Identity landscapes: Contemplating place and the construction of self* (pp. 185–196). Leiden, Netherlands: Brill Sense.

Ng-A-Fook, N. (Producer), & Brant-Birioukov, K. (Guest). (2020). Episode 11: Kiera Brant-Birioukov [Audio podcast]. *Fooknconversation.* Retrieved from https://www.fooknconversation.com/podcast/episode-11-kiera-brant-birioukov/.

Sabzalian, L. (2018). Curricular standpoints and native feminist theories: why native feminist theories should matter to curriculum studies. *Curriculum Inquiry, 48*(3), 359–382.

(Re)membering Indigenous Curriculum Theorists 129

Styres, S. (2017). Pathways for remembering and recognizing indigenous thought in education: Philosophies of iethi'nihsténha ohwentsia'kékha (land). Toronto: University of Toronto Press.

Todd, Z. (2016). An Indigenous feminist's take on the ontological turn: 'Ontology' is just another word for colonialism. *Journal of Historical Sociology, 29*(1), 4–22.

Tuck, E. (2011). Rematriating curriculum studies. *Journal of Curriculum and Pedagogy, 8*(1), 34–37.

Tuck, E., & Gaztambide-Fernández, R. A. (2013). Curriculum, replacement, and settler futurity. *Journal of Curriculum Theorizing, 29*(1), 72–89.

16 On My Knees
Embracing Adoption to Understand Curriculum

Dorothy Vaandering

April 17, 1997-Tuesday.
Tonight, we came home from kids' choir, I went through the front door, you to the back. Your door was locked so you rang the doorbell. I answered,
    Me: Well, hello there! Can I help you?
    You: Can I come in and you be my new family?
I was surprised. Though Christopher, your older brother, often played this type of game you have always kept thoughts of this sort very private. We continued playing with this idea of you coming into this "new" family and you repeatedly said you'd be happy here. When I put you to bed, we did Best Things:
    You: My best thing today is...my "new" family (giggle, giggle).
    I asked lots of other families. No one wanted me but you do!
    You be my family forever!
    Me: Yes, forever, Anthony.
How can I hug you enough?

[our parent-child journal]

April 17, 1997 was almost two years after Anthony became part of our family. He was four when he arrived, joining Christopher, his new brother, who had come three years earlier when he had just turned five. To my knowledge, Anthony would not be mimicking Chris, as Chris' knocking had occurred before Anthony joined us. I ponder this experience often, and though it is now 25 years after we became a family of four, I can still hear the doorbell ringing, opening the door to the child Gerald and I had committed to two years earlier, and hearing his request to "come in" reverberating through my flesh, bones, and soul.

When asked who has inspired my curriculum journey, after 20 years of teaching, three years of curriculum writing, seven years of graduate work, and now 11 years in my current position in the field of Curriculum Teaching and Learning, no one comes to mind more clearly than our two sons and no experience more significant than our family's shared reality of adoption.

DOI: 10.4324/9781003154112-17

I try to shake these for a more "academic" response, but at this moment, I know it is time for me to embrace adoption as my doorway to understanding curriculum.

Before tapping into its connection to curriculum, I acknowledge two significant factors in this learning. First, I have walked this path with my husband Gerald, an artist and educator, in the most intricate and intimate ways imaginable, recognizing fully that our understanding of education and living has come from grappling *together* with the complexities of life. Second, it is imperative to admit that embracing adoption was not easy for either of us. We did not choose it, it chose us out of necessity – out of a desire to have children when infertile. And though society, community, family, and my person try to applaud that decision with words like "You're doing such a noble thing," "How great that you are opening your home to children with complex needs," "How blessed your children are to have you," I now know these are empty, empty words and sentiments that drip with patronizing and repulsive sympathy for loss. They are simply a façade for the louder messages of, "Wow, are you sure you know what you are getting into?" or "Have you tried everything possible to get pregnant?" or the bus stop advertising campaign of the time that kicked me in the gut with each sighting screaming out "The years before five are critical!" Later, when the boys would get suspended from school or do less than admirable things in the community, I couldn't shake the internal and external unspoken messages of "Well, what did you expect?" or "This probably has something to do with their early lives." And when they did things well or now that they are adults, the equally disturbing messages of surprise, "Wow, they are really stable, wonderful human beings!" Carefully considering the inherent inferences contained within all of these attitudes is disturbing.

Why is this disturbing and what makes my admission imperative? Because I need to expose a way of thinking that is also embedded and hidden in much of the current, dominant understanding of curriculum. These attitudes are fraught with and rooted in colonialism – that I have the capacity to help the "unfortunate" while forgetting that I began my adoption journey with the selfish need to be a parent, that had we had biological children we would not have adopted. Ingrained in this way of thinking are the educational myths of teacher as expert, of curriculum as objective, of knowledge as definitive; those with the resources can infer that they know better than those without, and theirs is the responsibility to bestow on others, their insights. Oppressive power perpetuated gently and insidiously.

I am writing this chapter at a time when the coronavirus pandemic has scared us all into a realization that "we can see clearly now that no one can see clearly" (Vaandering, 2020). I am also writing on the Monday after George Floyd was murdered by a white police officer in Minneapolis and the weekend protests are rebirthing the civil rights movement in the United States while Canada continues to only

132 *Dorothy Vaandering*

whisper about its own genocidal lifestyle (Rohadi, 2020). This, combined with awakening to my children's vulnerability, and what that has taught me, is so visceral I sense myself collapsing to my knees with the question reverberating, "Why am I writing this chapter?"

Without my sons, without the experience of adoption, without being challenged and most often failing to love them unconditionally, I would not know so viscerally that curriculum is ultimately justice expressed as "honouring the worth and interconnectedness of all people and our environment" (Vaandering, 2010) and creating space for the unknown, *not* the known; where curriculum "may draw on any external discipline for methodological help but does *not* allow the methodology to determine inquiry" (Eigan, 2003, emphasis added).

In spite of the ongoing discussion in curriculum theory and practice encouraging openness, inquiry (Eigan, 2003), and complexity (Davis, Sumara, & Luce-Kapler, 2015), the willingness and ability to be comfortable in unknowing evade us in education as standardized testing continues to grip and direct learning. Like my failed attempts at unconditional love, so too, are my efforts as a teacher-educator who only occasionally succeeds at trusting her students to lead their learning, at creating spaces of hope where joy meets struggle (Palmer, 2017), where I let go of the "evaluative gaze" (Black, 2016).

This (e)motion of falling to my knees takes on more significance as I observe protesters take a knee for 8 minutes and 46 seconds in these weeks following George Floyd's homicide. Ironically, though symbolic of the police officer restricting life by placing his knee on Floyd's neck, the collective gesture of protesters is intended not as an honouring of all those who have needlessly died, but rather *how* these deaths, time and again, expose the reality of systemic racism, the reality of life being drained from those considered undeserving or less fortunate. On one knee, people mobilize around injustice, refusing to comply with systems that oppress, ready to rise and defend the rights of those harmed. On both knees, I am bent over immobilized, as I realize my incredible potential for seeking personal benefit over defending the humanity of others. On my knees, I am finally cognisant of the impact of my actions, penitent, and can rise when those I have conditionally accepted, reach out their hand to me, graciously accepting me for who I am.

And is this not the message of unconditional acceptance, of being honoured as worthy, as fully human, that which Indigenous, Black, and People of Colour have been advocating for decades now? Is this not the message children and youth who struggle to engage learning in traditional settings have been speaking loudly through their repeated suspensions, expulsions, and decisions to drop out of school? How often has the education system turned away from recommendations beyond accommodation to *re-forming* itself ensuring that *all* people see themselves reflected in their learning, in their opportunity to engage in inquiry relevant to their lives

On My Knees 133

and communities? Something systemic *and* something in me, as a person of privilege, have us returning again and again to what we know causes some people harm and others hope. Curriculum as process, as praxis, or as content, curriculum informed by complexity theory, developmental theory, or constructivist theory; whatever stance an educator takes, curriculum can be engaged with generously or with greed, it can cause harm or nurture life.

At this time in history, with all its complexity, pain, and turmoil, how has adoption informed my curriculum journey? I rest less in the definitions of knowledge and curriculum informed by various theories, and more in theologian Deitrich Bonhoeffer's (1959) insights. "Bewilderment is the true comprehension. Not to know where you are going is the true knowledge" (p. 47). Or novelist and environmental activist, Wendell Berry's (1983) revelation. "It may be that when we no longer know what to do, we have come to our real work, and when we no longer know which way to go, we have begun our real journey." When I can let go, then I can learn and be in deep, authentic, reciprocal relationship that reveals the wonder of life even in the midst of difficulties.

Gifts, grace, and gratitude come to me through the immense courage of two little boys who had to surrender all, who came to a time in their lives where they could knock on our door and ask, *Can I come in and you be my new family?* I opened the door each time surprised by their question and so thankful my sons were reaching in to me, helping me to accept that we had no idea what would unfold, only that we would work on it together. And I am grateful.

References

Berry, W. (1983). Standing by words, in *Our Real Work*. Counterpoint.

Black, C. (2016). *Children, learning, and the 'Evaluative Gaze' of school*. On-line essay: http://carolblack.org/the-gaze.

Bonhoeffer, D. (1959). *Cost of discipleship*. London: SCM Press.

Davis, B., Sumara, D., & Luce-Kapler, R. (2015). *Engaging minds*. New York, NY: Routledge.

Eigan, K. (2003). What is curriculum? *Journal of the Canadian Association of Curriculum Studies*, 1(1), 9–16.

Palmer, P. (2017). Hope is the place where joy meets struggle. On Being. Blog post. https://onbeing.org/blog/parker-palmer-hope-is-the-place-where-joy-meets-the-struggle/

Rohadi. (2020). *Uncovering racism and pathways to action*. Blog post. https://www.rohadi.com/2020/race-reconcile/reconciling-racism-pushing-conversation-part-1/.

Vaandering, D. (2010). The significance of critical theory for restorative justice in education. *The Review of Education, Pedagogy, and Cultural Studies*, 32(2), 145–176.

Vaandering, D. (2020). *We can see clearly now that we can't see clearly*. Blog post. https://www.relationshipsfirstnl.com/post/at-this-time-5-we-can-see-clearly-now-that-we-can-t-see-clearly.

17 Gratitude, Living, and Left Together ...

Robert Nellis

What is gratitude? What does it mean to me, and how has it moved my life? Merriam-Webster offers that it is "the state of being grateful: thankfulness" (Merriam-Webster, n.d.). Notwithstanding the sense of the notion as a state of being, I'd like to explore it as a practice, as something one does – as a kind of leaning towards something. I do not think of gratitude as an entirely passive, receptive state, but rather as inhering a sort of intention, which certainly opens towards a kind of being. And I think of that being as a being-with. Like many people, I undertake daily affirmations of appreciation and gratefulness for all of the blessings in my life: health, a steady job I enjoy, a beautiful world to live in – but especially the people in my life: students and colleagues, friends, and family. It occurs to me as I sit within a thankfulness space long enough that there is ever something outside of the horizon of my immediate awareness calling to me and making possible the very conditions of my gratitude: those who have gone before. Indeed, how anaemic and short-sighted would be my gratitude if I only considered those I could see with my eyes immediately before me. In a sense, this is gratitude in the long view. I recall the line by George Orwell (1949) that "the best books ... are those that tell you what you know already" (p. 253). It's not like this lesson of gratitude's long view has never been presented to me before, but perhaps it's *when the student is ready, the teacher will appear.*

One teacher who appeared for me in my life and for whom I feel profound gratitude was Professor Carl Leggo. I swear I have a memory of Professor Leggo saying something along the lines: "you know the thing about the Academy is if you stick around long enough, you eventually become part of it" (C. Leggo, personal communication, n.d.). I love and appreciate this sentiment for so many reasons, one of which is that it says something about the power of *being-with.*

Attending university for me was a site of being-with. I did not go right after high school, working for a good number of years first. What's the old line about, when you know the *why* the *how* will take care of itself? Like many, I had to face the question of why did I want to do this? How

DOI: 10.4324/9781003154112-18

did I link that journey with my deepest and most profound needs? To be honest, one of the needs that ached for me was the need for belonging. In a way, my studies had served as a pathway for this. Arguably, many times, the work itself took second place just to participate and be part of things, which worked fine for me. However, it was with a sense of alarm that I started seeing the end of my graduate school days getting closer and closer. For one thing, I think I quite understood how difficult was the job market. It was not guaranteed by any means that I was going to be able to find a position. At least when I was there on the path of study, I was in the space of belonging. I feared what might come next to be an abyss. It was on my last day ostensibly as a student, the day of my Ph.D. oral defence when I met Carl Leggo for the first time.

As is well known and sadly remembered in the Curriculum Studies community and beyond, Professor Leggo passed away on March 7, 2019. For the Canadian Society for the Study of Education conference in 2019, a pre-conference was organized to honour his work, life, and legacy. Entitled *The Many Faces of Love: Celebrating the Lifework of Carl Leggo*, the event was a "day of celebration and remembrance through creativity: Poetry, performance, and short papers, as well as visual displays" (CACS 2019 pre-conference, n.d.). The event itself was thoroughly rooted in gratitude, gratitude for a teacher and scholar of profound influence. I felt honoured to share the following piece on that day.

Won't you come in, we've been waiting for you ...

Do you ever start
reading a poem,
and not get past
the first line?

Not because you object
to the verse,
but because
you are not wanting
to finish,
unwilling

to leave
until
you know
for sure

it will be coming
with you?

136   Robert Nellis

I feel this says something about my sense of being-with my encounter with Professor Carl Leggo's life and work.

I feel that I may step away from the page and that I do so not leaving him behind, that in a sense, he comes with me. But not in a way that I presume to have him captured or contained. But that I can know, trust, that perhaps in a dream I'll feel a familiarity, ease. I'll look up from the page and return. And if I am to find him, undoubtedly others would as well. At this time, as before March 7, I feel Carl greets me. He greets me as one, admittedly, a singular, specific, particular figure, but also as more.

I think that as with many who have shared pedagogy with him, I've never forgotten him. Why I wonder? A story I tell myself is that he was a person who lived "yes." While so many take as their pedagogical role to say no, perhaps as the sculptor removes stone and debris around the sculpture, there are other ways to nurture and reveal the art within. I think this other direction points toward Carl's work. He breathed and shared an affirmative spirit, a living pedagogy of yes.

I remember back to the day when I first met him. The occasion of our meeting was his kind service as external examiner for my Ph.D. thesis oral defence in 2007. I entered the room that day, all nerves, anxiety, and rootlessness to find him sitting across the table all ponytail, beard, and warmth. Perhaps it's incorrect to say that I found him there – possibly better that I entered into his presence, an uncanny feeling of stillness, calm, peace. Although we had never met, I immediately felt as though I had known him forever. He radiated a pedagogy – but not of narrow instrumentalism – but one that dwells with and in a heart of affinity, a sense of being with, in, feeling with, attuned, sensitive – embodied and transcending, with and beyond. I found his to be a pedagogy of a kind of multiplicity, an embodied irony. I never felt quite sure what I would expect or anticipate with him, that he would simultaneously reassure and surprise, to reveal a sense of his "I," through and infused with the richness of its otherwises. Perhaps that might be a source of – in addition to his brotherly, fatherly care – also that sly twinkle. There is only one Professor Leggo, but that one is also so many. I recall the proverb when the student is ready the teacher will appear, and with Professor Leggo, I seem to hear him saying, won't you come in, we've been waiting for you ...

I feel so grateful for that sense of being with that sense of community, communion, and coming together. I think of this as a space of welcome,

Gratitude, Living, and Left Together ...   137

a space of inclusion, perhaps like the final scene from *Titanic* (Cameron, 1997) when Rose follows the necklace down through what at first appears to be a cold, empty hulk at the bottom of the sea. But when she enters it, she finds a warm space through doors opened by all those she remembers in smiles: *we've been waiting for you.* Maybe such a space is a space where within my own psychic life, those who have departed await: dear friends, parents, grandparents, beings named as pets, places, memories. To imagine this, to have such a space within, is a blessing.

But it is a difficult blessing, is it not? It is a blessing born of many of the most difficult and challenging times of life, times of loss. To see this as a space of gratitude comes with experience – perhaps aspirationally, very well leading towards wisdom, towards as I shall discuss, character.

Carl (Leggo, 2015) has discussed character through his encounter with James Hillman's *The Force of Character and the Lasting Life* (1999). In "Loving Language: A Poet's Vocation and Vision," he cites Hillman, "why *do* we live so long?" (as cited in Leggo, 2015, p. 147). He then suggests that "the last years confirm and fulfil character" (p. 147). He shares this as part of thinking about one's life, storying one's experience as a means to understand it. And to understand it as "a plural complexity, a multiphasic polysemous weave" (p. 32). Though the process of character involves putting in a sense one's life into a story, it does not do so in a neat and tidy way. It embraces life in its messiness, in its difficulty, in its heartbreak. In a sense, this becomes a space of character. Carl further draws on Hillman that he especially wants to ensure that the uniqueness of character does not yield to, for some, the tantalizing unity of a caricature (Leggo, 2015). It becomes crucial that character becomes a shared pathway with pain, as pain is part of a complete life. I would add that if one accepts this explanation, and if character becomes a desirable capacity, then it and its pathway become something for which one ought to practice and to lean into in gratitude.

Hillman had developed something of this theme and rooted it in that most profound journey for all living beings: death, or as he would prefer to frame it in the language of "leaving" and "left" (Hillman, 1999). For most people, one wants to live as long as possible and to do so in the richest, most fulfilling way with the utmost integrity. One wants to last as long as possible. We may wish to hold on often: to this moment, this love, this ever-fleeting beauty. However, that impulse inheres within it the very underlying character of fluidity, change, passing. Hillman (1999) writes, "the move from lasting to leaving changes our basic attitude from holding on to letting go" (p. 73). Part of wisdom, part of character becomes the realization that one can only yield to this process.

However, that yielding may be messier than one initially wishes to acknowledge. Have you ever found, getting to the end of a project, yourself called upon to draw more from your resources – strength perhaps not realizing you had – than you had ever imagined? What are those

138 *Robert Nellis*

lines from the Bruce Cockburn song that "nothing worth having comes without some kind of fight" (Cockburn, 1984), and that you've got to "kick at the darkness till it bleeds daylight" (1984)? Part of this calling upon resources relates towards Hillman's notion of leaving. Hillman writes, "before the body becomes a corpse in a casket it seems to have a lot to say to the soul" (Hillman, 1999, p. 121). And what is this message? What is this curriculum of leaving? I don't think I would want to say that it is the same message or lesson for everyone. As has been discussed above, part of this is the process of storying one's life. Perhaps a unifying message is the very structure rather than the content of the process. For Hillman, character is born of these unique challenges that people face: "where do they get their intelligence and vitality from, and their unique characters? From their troubles, their breakdowns" (p. 122). And a big part of this is living with loss, regardless of who that may be:

> Your mother, for instance—or a deceased husband, a lover, a teacher, a very dear friend, a person you knew only slightly—has left, and yet remains as a force of character (p. 171). In fact, that time and space can be the most powerful: "People's images survive their passing and, sometimes, have more power after they have left." (p. 171)

I had encountered this powerful sentiment earlier, this time by someone else I look up to with gratitude within the curriculum field: a former professor of mine from the University of Alberta: Dennis Sumara. He asked the question in seminar one day, "how long do parents live?" following that, "they live as long as their children do – because they live within them" (D. Sumara, personal communication, n.d.). To think of those who have passed away as still with me is a blessing for which I am grateful. When I think of all those I have loved and have gone ahead, passed away, died, this curiously does not weaken me, buckle my legs, and sap strength from me. Far from it! I live this awareness as offering quite the opposite experience. It gives me strength and grounding. It gives me the courage to, among other things, think of death and dying differently.

And Hillman (1999) offers a way to do precisely this: "suppose you exchange the word 'leaving' for 'dying'" (p. 171) and think of those who have died as left. I note how he pays special attention to the verb that we attach to "left" and draws upon the distinction between one who *has* left and one who *is* left. As I read it, the difference is that the second remains, that one can be gone and still remain. Here, "remains" operates not as a noun but as a verb. It differs from the more received, if macabre, thinking about those who have left as *remains*. Indeed, gratitude for me becomes the opportunity and blessing of living with those who are left. My dear loved ones *have* left but also *are* left, as am I – but not left behind. In gratitude, I feel left in front, left forward, left to the future, and left together …

References

CACS 2019 pre-conference: The many faces of love: Celebrating the lifework of Carl Leggo. (n.d.). Retrieved July 7, 2020, from https://educ.ubc.ca/celebrating-the-lifework-of-carl-leggo-csse-pre-conference/.

Cameron, J. (Director). (1997). *Titanic* [Film]. Hollywood, CA: Paramount Pictures.

Cockburn, B. (1984). Lovers in a dangerous time [Song]. In *Stealing fire*. New York, NY: Gold Mountain.

Hillman, J. (1999). *The force of character and the lasting life* [Kindle]. New York, NY: The Random House Publishing Group.

Leggo, C. (2015). Loving language: A poet's vocation and vision. In S. Walsh, B. Bickel, & C. Leggo (Eds.), *Arts-based and contemplative practices in research and teaching: Honouring presence* (pp. 141–168). New York, NY: Routledge.

Merriam-Webster. (n.d.). Gratitude. In Merriam-Webster.com *dictionary*. Retrieved July 6, 2020, from https://www.merriam-webster.com/dictionary/gratitude.

Orwell, G. (1949). *1984*. Planet Ebook. Retrieved from https://www.planetebook.com/free-ebooks/1984.pdf.

18 Coming into Being, Again and Again and Again

Avril Aitken

Our field then, is gifted with the presence of scholars who bring differing innovative theoretical and methodological ideas for us to listen to, reflect on, and synthesize in relation to our research methodologies, our theorizing, and in our praxis where the term "curriculum" still remains many things to many people. Our community of scholars and their "crazy" ideas is what comprises the distinct field of Canadian curriculum studies. Might we then continue to be open and pay attention, to live well together as a community without consensus.

(Ng-A-Fook, 2014, p. 44)

I have often thought of myself as an accidental curriculum studies scholar, given what feels like my late arrival to active participation in the community. Interestingly, another story emerged through writing this reflection. I discovered that my work was being influenced by such scholars well before I became aware that the community existed. Their words and actions inspired and deepened my thinking about the significance of the interior life to teaching and learning. In what follows, I pick up threads from different moments to bring forward names of those whose gifts shored me up and provoked my thinking over the years.

2003 – Coming into Being, Again

In October 2003, I invited a group of women to come together for a Thanksgiving weekend of reflection, discussion, and writing. A characteristic that tied them together, beyond career choice, was that, at one point in the previous 20 years, they had taught in one specific school in subarctic Canada, which served a First Nation. Some had never met but I knew each of them to a certain degree, having also taught in the community in question.

My dissertation emerged from the events of that autumn weekend, and while it might be considered a turning point, I believe it's better described as a pivotal moment of "rethinking," the kind called for by

DOI: 10.4324/9781003154112-19

Coming into Being, Again and Again and Again 141

Janet L. Miller. In writing about curriculum studies as a dynamic field, Miller points to the need for ongoing thinking about what "constrain[s] possibilities of new iterations of 'self' and 'other,'" and concludes, "this rethinking will require our field and ourselves to come into being, again and again, as that which we have yet to know" (Miller, 2010, p. 100). The notion of the continuous process of coming into being in the face of the unknown is well-matched to my journey.

By all accounts, 2003 was also an important year for curriculum studies in Canada. The first issue of the *Journal of the Canadian Association for Curriculum Studies* (JCACS) was published; the association (CACS) selected the first recipient of the *Ted T. Aoki Award for Distinguished Service within the Field of Canadian Curriculum Studies*; and Cynthia Chambers's (2003) oft-cited chapter, "'As Canadian as possible under the circumstances': A view of contemporary curriculum discourses in Canada" was published. These three events were in the making while my doctoral proposal was taking shape. It shows that I was working with ideas of anti-racist scholars and studies of whiteness. I had only begun to explore teachers' identity formation, as a result of crucial conversations with my supervisor, Judith Robertson, and fellow doctoral student, Linda Radford.

Classroom teaching preoccupied me, yet I was drawn to doctoral studies as a result of questions that kept me "awake at night," as Chambers (2004) would say. "What matters may lurk in that time in between sleep and wakefulness" (p. 9) – I was preoccupied by the prevalence of racist attitudes and materials that Indigenous students and their families routinely encountered in the subarctic school in which I had been teaching for just under two decades.

I moved north as soon as I completed my certifying degree in 1980. It wasn't a complicated decision. I am the first in my family to be born in Canada, so was relatively unrooted in this landscape. As a merchant marine, my father had followed Canada's coastal contours and with deep appreciation had sailed the St. Lawrence. When the opportunity to emigrate arose, he didn't hesitate. When a subarctic teaching opportunity presented itself, I didn't hesitate.

1990 – Towards Coming into Being

Unfortunately, it took too long for my common-sense beliefs about education to be disrupted. I misread the gracious hospitality of the members of the First Nations community as a reinforcement that my efforts were what they wanted for their children. I was naive, compounded by the fact that my undergraduate studies hadn't acknowledged Indigenous issues. Not surprisingly, I was unaware of the National Indian Brotherhood's (1972) seminal text, *Indian Control of Indian Education*. I am forever grateful that the students' voices cut

142   *Avril Aitken*

through my obliviousness. One day, when I had no meaningful answer for a student who asked, "Why do we have to go to school?" I realized that I had significant work to do.

In 1990, I registered in McGill's master's program. My first courses were with Claudia Mitchell and David Dillon, who found ways to support my part-time studies while I continued to teach. I shaped a new practice while juxtaposing the readings they suggested, and carrying out classroom-based critical action research in the subarctic. At Claudia's encouragement, my first article was published in *English Quarterly*. Through their courses and given the role they played as readers for my research, I grew in confidence as a thinker and a writer.

2003 – Coming into Being, Again – Part II

My master's led me to have a new resolve. I learned alongside my students as we read works by Indigenous authors: Jeanette Armstrong, Thomson Highway, Daniel David Moses, Beatrice Culleton, Lee Maracle, Thomas King, and Drew Hayden Taylor come quickly to mind. While somewhat unprepared, I moved with my family from the subarctic community in 1997 when my partner continued graduate studies. I had no idea what would follow, but seeking out a doctoral program seemed inevitable given the questions that dogged me.

Notably, as my doctoral inquiry was underway in October 2003, I was unaware of CACS and the existence of the association's journal. The overall arc of my proposal seems to show that I was headed in a direction away from the preoccupations of curriculum studies. Yet, a review of the contents of JCACS 1(1), released that year, signals something completely different. The articles that bookend the issue curiously nod to my future and my past. The first is written by Deborah Britzman (2003), whose writing my supervisor had just brought to my attention; while I didn't realize it at the time, Britzman's work would become the most inspiring for my thinking. It would become central to my practice and inquiries carried out with Linda Radford in the last decade. The closing article was written by Sandra Weber and Claudia Mitchell (2003), who had already contributed to shaping my thinking. There is enough magic in the way that these two articles appeared in that initial issue of JCACS to suggest that the field of curriculum studies would be on my radar at some point. However, even more synchronicity was afoot. Weber and Mitchell had been invited to muse on their experiences of collaborative work in curriculum studies; the editors commented on their submission in the introduction.

> [T]he site of their collaboration is all at-once geographical, intellectual, phenomenological, and cultural. Ideas spring not only from

Coming into Being, Again and Again and Again   143

academic debates but, as well, from practices of socializing (shared meals, shopping, traveling) and from rituals of friendship ... both identities and ideas emerge from tangled webs of interdependence ... these collusions can become both productive and pleasurable.

(Sumara & Luce-Kapler, 2003, p. 7)

I found it uncanny to read the article, given that contributions I have made in the field of curriculum studies have resulted from working closely with Linda Radford. She has been the co-investigator in many of the research-pedagogy projects I have undertaken since 2011. I believe that such working relationships are unusual; yet, if I had to find the words to describe what we have experienced over the years, they would be remarkably similar to what JCACS' editors wrote about Weber and Mitchell.

Highlanders, Inner Life, and Synchronicity

My mother, whose roots are in the Scottish highlands, would occasionally remind me and my sister that members of our family may be "fey." Her comments would generally be accompanied with stories of clairvoyance and suggestions that we should be watchful for its manifestation in our lives. She also cautioned us not to draw attention to ourselves; early in my life, this translated into listening carefully (rather than speaking) and observing well. My father was a lowlander who grew up near a river that led him out to sea. From that beloved location, he would spend long stretches of time watching the horizon. Before his untimely death at a young age, I learned to appreciate the importance of keeping your gaze on what lies beyond perception.

For most of my life, I have wondered about the significance of interior life; I would say it's no accident that I have this preoccupation.

2010 – Coming into Being, Again and Again – This Time in Community

It seems odd to me now that I didn't have a concrete plan for what might follow completion of my Ph.D.; I continued supporting school-based research, sponsored by the Ministry of Education, and made repeated trips north to contribute to initiatives in the community where I had taught. It wasn't long until a ministry colleague nudged me towards university.

In the fall 2010, I invited Linda Radford to speak to students in a graduate course in academic reading and writing that I was teaching. Soon after, we began working in the same teacher education program. We shared the space of a small farmhouse several nights a week, which provided ample opportunities for pulling apart questions about

144　*Avril Aitken*

subjectivity, the unconscious, and the struggles of becoming teachers. We took up filmmaking in the teacher education classroom as a form of research-pedagogy. It was the beginning of what Sumara and Luce-Kapler describe, as "identities and ideas emerg[ing] from tangled webs of interdependence" (2003, p. 7).

Sharing physical spaces enhances a sense of belonging. The 5th Biennial Provoking Curriculum Conference in Edmonton in October 2011 provided an important moment through which I identified with a community of scholars "who bring differing innovative theoretical and methodological ideas for us to listen to, reflect on, and synthesize in relation to our research methodologies" (Ng-A-Fook, 2014, p. 44). It was the first time that Linda and I presented together. Judith Robertson provided an introduction to the papers we presented along with Nectaria Karagiosis, another of her students: *Vulnerable sites and guises: Studies of adult symbolizing experiences in three venues of education*. From that point forward, Linda and I continued to collaborate, despite her move to another university. Within a year of Provoking Curriculum, I had met many other members of the community and joined the executive of CACS. I'm grateful to Nicholas Ng-A-Fook for nudging me to get involved, and for the many ways he lives and builds community. I eventually shared the co-presidency with Teresa Strong-Wilson, whose generous mentoring and friendship sustained me through the labours of leadership, conference chairing, guest-editing JCACS, and many other undertakings.

2013 – Again and Again and Again – In Community

It was Teresa who brought together a group of five women scholar/ teacher educators for regular meetings in 2013. We worked closely with Pinar and Grumet's (2015) seminal text, *Toward a Poor Curriculum* and carried out a *currere* practice, which was first published in 1976.

> We gathered as sojourners: itinerants enjoying the solace of one another's company along the way—along life's way. We were not a committee struck for an institutional purpose, nor a cross-university collaboration oriented towards garnering funds or sharing results ... We read, we discussed, we wrote, we shared what we wrote, we assembled our writings and invited one another to respond.
>
> (Strong-Wilson et al., 2019, p. 9)

This collective experience was profoundly intimate and restorative; it allowed for critical reflection, new perspectives, and a deeper commitment to understanding the significance of interior life and the unconscious to teaching and learning.

"Be Open and Pay Attention" – Coming into Being, Again and Again and Again

Linda Radford and I have elsewhere described our inquiry-based approach as an attempt to work against notions of fixed identities and knowledge, and rigid imaginations of transformation and outcome-focused models of education. It's how we move forward within and against the highly regulated world of teacher certification, which routinely ignores the preoccupations of curriculum studies scholarship. It takes courage to sustain the energy and commitment to living out these tensions in university settings that are increasingly shaped by neoliberal agendas. Community can sustain us and curriculum studies scholars – given their innovative theories and methodologies – are well equipped to support each other in the face of moments like the ones we are currently living. It's a particularly important time to "be open and pay attention" (Ng-A-Fook, 2014, p. 44). I am grateful to members of the CACS community who have inspired and supported that stance. And I am particularly grateful for the long relationship of learning that continues with members of the Naskapi Nation who first greeted me four decades ago. Without them, I might not have met the three remarkable curriculum studies scholars who turned up in my life, around the beginning of each of the decades that followed: Claudia Mitchell, Linda Radford, and Teresa Strong-Wilson. Given that it's 2020, my eyes are on the horizon for my next guide.

References

Britzman, D. (2003). Five excursions into free association, or just take the A train. *Journal of the Canadian Association for Curriculum Studies, 1*(1), 25–37.

Chambers, C. (2003). 'As Canadian as possible under the circumstances': A view of contemporary curriculum discourses in Canada. In W. F. Pinar (Ed.), *The internationalization handbook of curriculum research* (pp. 221–252). Mahwah, NJ: Lawrence Erlbaum.

Chambers, C. (2004). Research that matters: Finding a path with heart. *Journal of the Canadian Association for Curriculum Studies, 2*(1), 1–19.

Miller, J. L. (2010). Response to Rubén A. Gaztambide-Fernandez: Communities without consensus. In E. Malewski (Ed.), *Curriculum studies handbook: The next moment* (pp. 95–100). New York, NY: Routledge.

National Indian Brotherhood/Assembly of First Nations. (1972). *Indian Control of Indian Education.* Retrieved from http://www.oneca.com/IndianControlofIndianEducation.pdf.

Ng-A-Fook, N. (2014). Provoking the very "idea" of Canadian curriculum studies as a counterpointed composition. *Journal of the Canadian Association for Curriculum Studies, 12*(1), 10–69.

Pinar, W., & Grumet, M. (2015). *Toward a poor curriculum,* 3rd ed. Kingston, NY: Educator's International Press.

146 *Avril Aitken*

Strong-Wilson, T., Yoder, A., Aitken, A., Chang-Kredl, S., & Radford, L. (2019). Currere tales: Journeying as pilgrims to the (an)archive. In T. Strong-Wilson, C. Ehret, D. Lewkowich & S. Chang-Kredl (Eds.), *Making/unmaking through provoking curriculum encounters* (pp. 9–18). New York, NY: Routledge.

Sumara, D., & Luce-Kapler, R. (2003). Inventing new vocabularies for curriculum studies in Canada. *Journal of the Canadian Association for Curriculum Studies*, *1*(1), 1–8.

Weber, S., & Mitchell, C. (2003). Collaboration and coauthorship: Reflections from the inside. *Canadian Association for Curriculum Studies*, *1*(1), 83–91.

19 From a Steel Town Down
Gifts, Grace and Gratitude
Adam Garry Podolski

Introduction

> *My love is like a pitbull terrier*
> *Forged, like steel*
> *from a steel town*

Image 19.1 Illustration by Adam Garry Podolski, Terrier & Blast Furnace, 2020: Graphite on paper.

DOI: 10.4324/9781003154112-20

148 *Adam Garry Podolski*

I come to this chapter as a young researcher, sharing aspects of my past that help me find and name the curricular gifts I am living. I name gifts that are helping me mature in my personal and professional life. To traverse an educational landscape in the context of myself-experiencing-the-world, I use the tradition of narrative inquiry put forth by Clandinin and Connelly (1994, 2000) along with William Pinar's (1994, 2011, 2015) method of *currere*.

To bring past constructions of experiential learning to praxis, Clandinin and Connelly (1994) note that in storying experience, an inquiry moves towards internal conditions – feelings, hopes and the moral disposition of the storyteller, who also looks at the existential conditions of their environment to bring to consciousness a temporal perspective by connecting the past to the present. Clandinin and Connelly state that, "To experience an experience is to experience it simultaneously in these four ways [inward, outward, backward, forward] and to ask questions pointing each way" (p. 417).

I also reflect on my personal experience keeping Pinar's (1994, 2011) method of *currere* in mind. Pinar (1994) describes *currere* as, "one way to work to liberate one from the web of political, cultural and economic influences that are perhaps buried from conscious view but nonetheless comprise the living web that is a person's biographic situation" (p. 108).

Growing up in a Steel Town Down

My story begins in a northern Ontario town, in the twilight of a golden age of an industry, with a steel plant in and out of bankruptcy. As a Canadian teenager, I found myself reckoning with the "gift" of globalization. In my steel industry town, globalization was not received as a beacon of progress, but ushered in what television program director Shawney Cohen's (2018) W5 and Vice documentary *Steel Town Down* director described as,

> The one place that felt a little hopeless. [Cohen goes on to say] there's a disconnect between generations and with so many economic needs, drug addiction has almost no profile. There's only one harm reduction officer for the whole city and five overdoses every day.
> (Canada's opioid crisis, 2018)

Introduced by W5's Kevin Newman, the documentary covers the shortage of job opportunities and a growing addiction epidemic in my hometown.

In a place not devoid of joy, where I lived, globalization arrived in the form of an economic grim reaper, leaving in its wake a buffet of illicit substances, which for many people made the socio-economic aftermath hell every day. The conditions in the neighbourhoods in my steel town

From A Steel Town Down   149

began my education, which in some ways was an unfortunate place to learn. However, my early years prepared me to work with some of the most extraordinary students I work with now, helping to forge my current resolve in my role as a Student Success Secondary School Teacher. I believe the students I currently learn with have recognized that I care deeply about the consequences of alcohol, drugs and economic disparity because of my personal relationship with each of these in my own story.

For me, the gift of gratitude comes from consciously moving towards health in my early years. This meant begrudgingly recognizing who and what I had to move away from. There were many kind and beautiful people, friends even, that, although I had respect for them in many ways, I judged them as I chose to move towards the people and places that would allow me to sustain a way of being that led to a healthy life. Looking back, I can say that it took courage, as a young person, to judge my surroundings and the people around me, not in a way that provided me with advice to give, or had me telling – becoming a telling expert – but in a way that left me caring deeply about the consequences of embracing a way of life that is self-destructive.

Gifts of Being – From Curriculum Theory, Philosophy and Biography

Being has a long legacy. When I contemplate the mix of genes gifted to me from my parents, I think of how unlikely the probability is/was of my parents meeting, and their parents, and so on, along that line of ancestry. Out of all possible futures, an unimaginable trajectory, an improbable lineage, had to occur, surviving across countless generations. It is hard to fathom how unlikely the gift of life is. As a practice, every day, I wake up, and I think about the unborn people – those who'll never wake up, and I think about how precious life is. I work to remember how lucky I am to be alive. I aim to practice being grateful in this way each day before I die.

In my master's research (Podolski, 2010) and doctoral dissertation (Podolski, 2018), I made the case that academically, intellectual ideas, like their genetic counterparts, are inherited. I trace the building blocks of my epistemological stance from scholars like Hegel (1807/1967) to John Dewey (1938), from Heidegger (1927/1996) to Ted Aoki (2005a, 2005b, 2005c, 2005d). For example, Dewey's (1938) focus on experiential learning, and his idea that a person is both social and individual was influenced by Hegel's (1807/1967) notion that what we do to develop ourselves develops society as a whole – minus Hegel's obsession with the absolute – a predetermined destination. Husserl (1900–1901/2008) and Heidegger's (1927/1996) focus on essence and contextually dependent *Being* influenced the renowned Canadian curriculum theoretician Ted Aoki's (2005a, 2005b, 2005c, 2005d) emphasis on life in the

150   *Adam Garry Podolski*

classroom. Ted Aoki then re-tuned the notion of curriculum to a teacher's conscious concern for the irreducibly unique qualities that individual students bring to a classroom; their scares, their freckles and the person-to-person-world-relationship that is the heart of curriculum.

From Pinar (1994, 2011, 2012, 2015), I inherited the gift of study and theorizing based on an exercise of investigating seminal life experiences while reviewing them through an academic lens. Shields (2005), along with Pinar (1994), explain that academic knowledge takes us far but must be connected to one's own tacit knowledge and brought to praxis. These ideas are gifts I apply daily in my professional practice.

Tacit Wisdom and Its Role in My Professional Practice

From Shields (2005, 2019) and Pinar (1994), I learned that gifts come from reflecting on my biographic situation. When thinking about my upbringing, I question what led me past the now undesirable habits that my younger self associated with "respect." As a teenager, in my steel town, I saw respect akin to promiscuous conquests, fighting, smoking and drinking. What gift(s) led me away from this mindset? Maybe it was luck, parenting, waking up to the beauty of the Great White North; or was I struck by the numerous examples that highlighted the hapless consequences of alcoholism, violence and other vices?

After taking several lessons on the chin, having been charged with assault at 14, I realized I moved in circles that limited me. To mature, I had to re-conceptualize my understanding of respect. I began treating my health, my mind and my body, better. I also became critical of the people closest to me. I applied critical theory, not as a formulaic expression of text compiled from philosophic texts, but from my judgement, unwelcomingly gifted from reflecting on my folly and failures and the failed philosophies of those trying to cope in my neighbourhood. I found valuable educational gifts in the low rental neighbourhoods in my town, received by thinking deeply about the deaths of friends. I learned from the example of those trying to escape from *a Steel Town Down*. I began to view death as a teacher.

It Became So Clear – It Should Have Been Obvious

After a number of intelligent people were unable to negotiate a future where I lived, I knew I could no longer acquiesce as a spectator. I measured the types of behaviours that I believed led to my friends' deaths. A philosophic perspective that glorifies drinking, macho-riotousness and its non-reflective "glory" should not be respected as normal or part of a tradition of growing up in a steel town. Such a perspective was an unchecked way of thinking adopted by many young people who struggled there,

From A Steel Town Down 151

myself included. I believe now my thinking involved a desire to close my eyes, to bull through. Looking back, I can say the qualities I held were tough, honest, but brash too. All that helped because if you didn't have much, people tended to laugh, but they wouldn't laugh if they were afraid. But they were afraid because you were vulnerable – and like any creature, there is fight or flight. Flight may have been an escape through drugs, or perhaps, from judging the habits and behaviours that were defining you. Fight led to being damaged, charged, trapped, hurt and limits life.

Cruelly Honest

I learned to resent the way of being described above. And I still wonder if adopting such a philosophy was simply part of growing up in a Steel Town Down. But, by assuming such beliefs, I embodied a philosophy of stagnation, of sameness, static-ness and devolution, of pride of place and of reputation.

From the more embarrassing aspects of my past, I have received wisdom – wisdom that is not grounded in pride, but in humility, in an element of my existence, which, I imagine some may snicker at or would consider humiliating. But it is in my weakness, and from my ignorance, melancholy and mourning, that I have found my greatest gifts. I judge the people I grew up with, the people that passed away. I judge myself, who I was during those years.

Wisdom came from growing up where and the way I did. I think wisdom comes from knowing the consequences of actions. Addiction and death were consequences I witnessed. Now I have knowledge that comes without pride – which is a gift. My wisdom is intimately coupled with my embarrassment. My embarrassment is sister to my compassion, and my compassion is responsible for how I've learned to express grace. I try to offer grace in my interactions with the students I work with in my Student Success role, especially when I work with students who are making unhealthy decisions. My stance, my practice, is founded in the wisdom I have gained, in my learning from stupid, preventable mistakes. It is not derived from intelligence in the academic sense, but from heart-swelling examples that have come from my life.

Although the unwanted lessons of my youth define the legacy of my learning, I cannot help but be conscious of the gratitude and grace I have been gifted from the people and places within a Steel Town Down. I would like to share that there is an extent to which normalized, insensitive bravado can become so deeply ingrained that it acts as philosophic concrete.

As I work through my past, I am lifted towards the bittersweet self-knowledge that brings my practice towards maturity, towards grace, towards my students, and the surface again. Although I am thankful for the gifts, grace and gratitude that come from self-study, *currere* and inquiry, in a way, I can't help but hold a grudge against them.

152　*Adam Garry Podolski*

References

Aoki, T. (2005a). Humiliating the Cartesian ego. In W. Pinar & R. Irwin (Eds.), *Curriculum in a new key: The collected works of Ted T. Aoki* (pp. 291–300). New York, NY: Routledge.

Aoki, T. (2005b). Inspiriting the curriculum. In W. Pinar & R. Irwin (Eds.), *Curriculum in a new key: The collected works of Ted T. Aoki* (pp. 361–365). New York, NY: Routledge.

Aoki, T. (2005c). Reflections of a Japanese Canadian teacher experiencing ethnicity. In W. Pinar & R. Irwin (Eds.), *Curriculum in a new key: The collected works of Ted T. Aoki* (pp. 333–348). New York, NY: Routledge.

Aoki, T. (2005d). Teaching as in-dwelling between two curriculum worlds. In W. Pinar & R. Irwin (Eds.), *Curriculum in a new key: The collected works of Ted T. Aoki* (pp. 159–165). Mahwah, NJ: Lawrence Erlbaum.

Canada's opioid crisis spreading to smaller communities that struggle to cope. (2018, February). CTV News. Retrieved from https://www.ctvnews.ca/w5/canada-s-opioid-crisis-spreading-to-smaller-communities-that-struggle-to-cope-1.3795223.

Clandinin, D. J., & Connelly, F. M. (1994). Personal experience methods. In N. K. Denzin & Y. S. Lincoln (Eds.), *Handbook of qualitative research* (pp. 413–427). Thousand Oaks, CA: Sage.

Clandinin, D. J., & Connelly, F. M. (2000). *Narrative inquiry: Experience and story in qualitative research*. San Francisco, CA: Jossey-Bass.

Cohen, S. (Director). (2018). Steel town down: Overdose crisis in the Soo. [TV Episode]. In R. Archibald, A. Koschany, & P. McGuire (Executive producers), *W5*. Canada: Vice Studio Canada.

Dewey, J. (1938). *Experience & education. The Kappa Delta Pi lecture series*. New York, NY: Collier.

Hegel, G. W. F. (1967). *The phenomenology of mind* (J. B. Baillie, Trans.). New York, NY: Harper & Row. (Original work published 1807).

Heidegger, M. (1996). *Being and time* (J. Stambaugh, Trans.). Albany: State of New York Press. (Original work published 1927).

Husserl, E. (2008). *Logical investigations* (J. N. Findlay, Trans.). New York, NY: Routledge. (Original work published 1900–1901).

Pinar, W. F. (1994). *Autobiography, politics and sexuality: Essays in curriculum theory 1972–1992*. New York, NY: Peter Lang.

Pinar, W. F. (2011). *The character of curriculum studies: Bildung, currere, and the recurring question of the subject*. New York, NY: Palgrave Macmillan.

Pinar, W. F. (2012). *What is curriculum theory?* (2nd ed.), New York, NY: Routledge.

Pinar, W. F. (2015). *Educational experience as lived: Knowledge, history, alterity: The selected works of William F. Pinar*. New York, NY: Routledge.

Podolski, A. (2010). *Building a teacher identity: An introspective view based on Charles Darwin's theory of natural selection*. Unpublished master's thesis, Nipissing University, North Bay, Ontario, Canada.

Podolski, A. (2018). *Towards a personal philosophy of curriculum, approaching currere and narrative inquiry within an Aokian paradigm of reciprocity*. Unpublished doctoral dissertation, Nipissing University, North Bay, Ontario.

Shields, C. (2005). Using narrative inquiry to inform and guide our (re)interpretations of lived experience. *McGill Journal of Education (MJE)*, *40*(1), 179–188.

Shields, C. (2019). The power of curriculum as autobiographical text: Insights from utilizing narrative inquiry self-study in research, teaching, and living. In C. Hébert, N. Ng-A-Fook, A. Ibrahim, & B. Smith. (Eds.), *Internationalizing curriculum studies: Histories, environments, and critiques* (pp. 177–189). New York, NY: Palgrave Macmillan.

20 Revisiting Place
The Gift of Lingering in a Curricular Legacy

Carmen Shields

Only in fairy tales,
or given freakish luck, does the wind
rise suddenly and set you down where everything
is safe and loved and in its place. The mind
does not expect it. But the heart,
the heart –
the heart keeps looking for itself.
It knows and does not know
where it belongs. (p. 37–40)
From 'Transparence' in Songs for Relinquishing the Earth
(Jan Zwicky, 1998)

Introduction

As a narrative inquirer and researcher of many years, I have often written about events and situations that comprise curricular experience (Guiney Yallop & Shields, 2016; Shields, 2005, 2019; Shields & Reid-Patton, 2009; Shields et al., 2011), but in this chapter, I turn to another aspect of remembrance important to narrative researchers, *place*, as I think again about two locations where, at the age of 24, I found myself newly single and alone, making decisions by myself for the first time. This was a time of recovery for me, recovery from the turbulence of trying to live a scripted and settled life that previously I had chosen to live. I had places to stay in my new province then but no home. But one day, thanks to the serendipity of the moment or "freakish luck," I came upon a village I had never seen before and immediately had a sense that I had found a place where I might belong.

At that same time, although I had no plans for my future, on a crisp September day chance found me on a university campus for the first time where I found my way to the Registrar's office and after being invited for morning tea with the Registrar, I gained entrance as a mature student. I had until Christmas to prove that I was capable of holding my own in classes that were already underway. From my new home, I travelled

DOI: 10.4324/9781003154112-21

Revisiting Place 155

across country to the campus three days a week to attend my chosen classes. With a set schedule that helped me begin a path to a more normal routine, subject matter to absorb that I found fascinating, and three friends, two of them new ones, to share life with in a house in my new village, my life slowly began to take shape in my own hands.

These two places grounded me and provided a rite of passage for me to begin a self-conscious, self-aware existence. Gradually, I built a base from which to travel forward. I began to heal from old failures and broken relationships and extend myself in new ways. Chance or luck seemed to be at work on my behalf then and I was able to open my heart and mind to my new experiences and revel in them. I linger in the legacy of these two places often these days as I come to the end of my career as a teacher and academic. I wonder where I might be now without the rich and meaningful experiences provided by the gift of dwelling in these places.

Sharing Stories of These Two Places

A Glimpse of the House at Petite Riviere

I was in my early twenties when I drove my second-hand Volkswagen beetle over a hill on my way to visit an old school friend from home for the weekend. There, spread out before me was a small, quaint, historic village with the Atlantic Ocean sparkling in the sun close by. It was breathtaking. Immediately, a sense of lightness came over me – happiness, I recognized – after the many months of upheaval and just getting by. Shortly after my first visit, I joined three others living in the house in the small village of Petite Riviere where I lived for a number of months.

Living there then seemed like a place out of time. It was a village settled in 1632, so much older than I was used to in my previous province. The old house was charming with large rooms full of light. I remember the windows had transparent, frilly white curtains that tied back on each side in the living room and dining room. There was a den off the dining room filled with books and I loved that I could see the ocean as I sat working at the table in my bedroom.

Entertainment was a beach walk, tea in the evening, our 1970's music playing. Living in Petite was a time of peace and quiet that left me strong again, and as I write this story, I realize there are so many stories I could share about those days that can inform me still. For now I can say that there was vibrancy in the days spent there, a lightness of spirit and a sense of waking up to myself as an individual in the world. The house and the memories remain vivid – the people, the colours of the days.

Eventually two of the people who lived with me there moved to Prince Edward Island and one became the geologist on the Ocean Ranger, an

156   Carmen Shields

oilrig that went down with all hands off the coast of Newfoundland on February 15, 1982. He was 28 years old. He is in my dreams, still a part of my life. As for me, I moved nearer to my university to complete my studies, eventually remarrying and raising two daughters. But I always returned to Petite in summer when my children were growing up, and now I spend much of the year in my own house nearby. Petite is the place that always draws me back – my centre is there – I walk the beach and breath the ocean air now just as I did back then. It brings me to myself as no other place does.

Being Embraced by Studious Others in a University Community

I had forgotten how much I loved much of my high school learning until I ventured into my first week of classes at the university as a mature student and sat listening to my Religious Studies professor – soon to be mentor – mesmerized by both the course content and the delivery, which he offered seemingly without effort. There were not many of us in the room – Religious Studies was a small department. My History classes were much larger, but luckily my two female professors were also captivating and I listened transfixed as they lectured. These three individuals opened doors for learning for me that I did not know existed prior to finding myself in that place. These three classes were of course part of the university, part of the town, part of the place that cradled me and allowed me to grow and develop as a person and a scholar. In my mind's eye, I see the town as it was then; the campus, the professors I studied with as they were long ago. While that particular time has passed and two of those marvelous individuals have passed away, the legacy of those years that lives in me is current, rich, and still instructive.

Curricular Gifts Given and Received

A Narrative View

I am not sure at this point in my life how many times I have shared Connelly and Clandinin's (1988; Clandinin, 2013) view that curriculum is comprised of all of life's experience – it has been my mantra as a professor of curriculum studies since I first understood it in the early 1990s in Michael Connelly's graduate classroom. One of Mick's many gifts to me was to understand that by looking back on specific seminal events, experiences, situations, and places, it is possible to gain new insights into the paths we have travelled, the influences we have absorbed, and how we can utilize that knowledge in our present and as we travel forward in time. Adding to this life-changing gift, Bill Pinar's description of curriculum as *currere* (Pinar, 1994, 2015), an ongoing and active

Revisiting Place 157

personal process, opened my eyes to my own autobiography as a source of learning – it is here that I make new meaning as I go forward, adding present-day experience to consider along with earlier ones.

In narrative terms, I remember the social worlds offered by the two special life-giving places I write about here – the people and our daily interactions, the temporal nature of life – the places themselves glow in my mind's eye. These aspects of narrative inquiry, the three-dimensional inquiry space described by Clandinin and Connelly (2000); and Clandinin, (2013), provide a way for me to conjure the past and see it now, in my present-day life.

Re-reading an article by Chambers (2008), I find another rich and meaningful way to think about these two places. With the help of Ingold (2000), Chambers describes a three-dimensional territory comprised of land, water, and sky, all of which are sources of nourishment – "they feed human beings with knowledge, spirit, and … sustenance" (p. 116). Chambers adds: "People receive nourishment from particular places and the inhabitants of those places … And as they learn and practice the skills necessary to live in [those] particular place(s) they [continue to] become who they are" (p. 117). While Chambers and I are writing about different times, people, and places, her words mean so much to me as I reflect on how I began again on land I did not know before, having never seen a Canadian coast nor as a city dweller, ever really attended to the big sky under which all occurrences take place.

Place Provides a Multi-Faceted Legacy

Like hook's (1990) description of place as she writes about being in her grandparent's house, "… the warmth and comfort of shelter, the feeding of our bodies, the nurturing of our souls …" (p. 41), my memory holds a sense of the sanctuary I found in these two places. I experienced an awakening in all my senses. Driving my old Volkswagen between home and university, I watched the almost empty landscape turn from ocean to small orderly town, the trees and small lakes along the way marking my passage. The smell of the ocean, the bodily experience of walking the beach by myself, the feel of shells I collected in my hands. The wind, the gulls – feeling my heart open and respond emotionally and spiritually to these environments – all are there in memory and are tangible in the present. I feel I can reach out and touch these places as they were then, so real does that time in my life seem to me still.

Breathing in acceptance along with the open spaces that surrounded me was like living in the fairy tale that Zwicky describes in her poem above. Gradually, in the coming and going between home and university, a sense of safety and security in my new life emerged and I began to feel a desire to step again into the broader world, taking what I was learning with me to offer others. Huggan (2003) writes: "There are places on the

158   *Carmen Shields*

planet we belong and they are not necessarily where we are born. If we are lucky – if the gods are in a good mood – we find them, for whatever length of time is necessary for us to know that, yes, we belong to the earth and it to us. Even if we cannot articulate this intense physical sensation, even if language fails us, we know what home is then, in our very bones" (p. 4). Her vision speaks volumes to me – I experienced such a sense of belonging in these two places in my new province, as if some part of me had been waiting there to be found.

Conclusion

I have a colleague and close friend who does not believe that everything happens for a reason. Rather, he believes in serendipity – the chance encounter, destiny, fate that guides us along our way. Reflecting back now, I think that I experienced serendipity first hand in my move to these places that have provided me with a world I would otherwise never have encountered. When I spend time at Petite Riviere now, walking the long and except for summer, mostly empty beach, I look at the hills that rise above the village where I once picked rosehips for cold weather tea, and I feel I am a part of the place itself – the land, the water, and the sky. I am also mindful that without my initial acceptance at the university, I would not have had these wonderful years of teaching and writing that have made my life so rich and full.

Here lies the heart of meaningful learning: ongoing engagement with where we have been provides us with a way of conceiving our present and future. Through a process of reconstruction, we are able to savour the places and people who have touched us and made an impact on our lives. My curricular decisions are not isolated from the places I have written about here, but are connected to all the events and situations I have lived. This is our curricular legacy – we carry our past into the present, and we can use it to plot our way forward as we live into the future. It is there that the heart waits to find itself and flourish.

References

Chambers, C. (2008). Where are we? Finding common ground in a curriculum of place. *Journal of the Canadian Association for Curriculum Studies, 6*(2), 113–128.

Clandinin, D. J., & Connelly, F. M. (2000). *Narrative inquiry: Experience and story in qualitative research.* San Francisco, CA: Jossey-Bass.

Clandinin, D. J. (2013). *Engaging in narrative inquiry.* Walnut Creek, CA: Left Coast Press.

Connelly, F. M., & Clandinin, D. J. (1988). *Teachers as curriculum planners: Narratives of experience.* New York, NY: Teachers College Press.

Revisiting Place 159

Guiney Yallop, J. J. & Shields, C. (2016). The poetics of relationship: Thinking through pedagogy across time using narrative inquiry self-study and poetic inquiry. In N. Ng-A-Fook, G. Reis, and A. Abrahim (Eds.), *Provoking curriculum studies: Strong poetry and the art of the possible in education*. New York: Routledge 41–55.

hooks, b. (1990). *Yearnings: Race, gender, and cultural politics*. Toronto, ON: Between the Lines.

Huggan, I. (2003). *Belonging: Home away from home*. Toronto, ON: Vintage Canada.

Ingold, T. (2000). *The perception of the environment: Essays in livelihood, dwelling, skill*. New York, NY: Routledge.

Pinar, W. F. (1994). *Autobiography, politics and sexuality*. New York, NY: Peter Lang.

Pinar, W. F. (2015). *Educational experience as lived*. New York, NY: Routledge.

Shields, C. & Reid-Patton, V. (2009). A curriculum of kindness: (Re) creating and nurturing heart and mind through teaching and learning. *Brock Education*, *18*(2), Spring issue, 4–15.

Shields, C., Novak, N., Marshall, B., & Guiney Yallop, J. J. (2011). Providing visions of a different life: self-study narrative inquiry as an instrument for seeing ourselves in previously unimagined places. Narrative Works: Issues, Investigations and Interventions, *1*(1), 63–77.

Shields, C. (2005). Using narrative inquiry to inform and guide our (re)interpretations of lived experience. *McGill Journal of Education (MJE)*, *40*(1), 179–188.

Shields, C. (2019). The power of curriculum as autobiographical text: Insights from utilizing narrative inquiry self-study in research, teaching, and living. In C. Hébert, N. Ng-A-Fook, A. Ibrahim, & B. Smith. (Eds.), *Internationalizing curriculum studies: Histories, environments, and critiques* (pp. 177–189). New York, NY: Palgrave Macmillan

Zwicky, J. (1998). *Songs for relinquishing the earth*. London, ON: Brick Books.

Index

Note: *Italicized* pages refer to figures.

AAACS *see* American Association for the Advancement of Curriculum Studies (AAACS)
Adichi, C. N. 120
AERA *see* American Educational Research Association (AERA)
affect theory 29
Aitken, A. 6, 140
alter-ego 56
American Association for the Advancement of Curriculum Studies (AAACS) 54
American Educational Research Association (AERA) 54; Narrative and Research SIG 80
ancestral ways of knowing 30–32
Ansu-Kyeremeh, K. 111
Antone, E. 111
Antone, G. 111
Antress, L. 67
Anusara yoga 69
Aoki, T. T. 3, 4, 14–16, 27, 32, 47, 52, 60, 80, 93–95, 127, 149–150; *Curriculum in a new key: The collected works of Ted T. Aoki* 10; geo-metrons as survivance 92
Apffel-Marglin, F. 92, 93, 95
Archibald, J. 110, 111, 113
Armstrong, J. 142
A/r/tography 89
ARTS *see* Arts Researchers and Teachers Society (ARTS)
Arts Researchers and Teachers Society (ARTS) 13
Ashenfelter, H.: *158 Saxophone Exercises* 78
Ayers, W. 65

Back, L.: *The Auditory Culture Reader* 80
Badiou, A. 108
Baergen, P. L.: *Tracing Ted Tetsuo Aoki's Intellectual Formation* 14
Bakhtin, M. M. 102–103
Ball, F. 78
Bank, M. 78
Barad, K. 29, 93
Barnhardt, R. 112
Barone, T. 27, 32
Basso, K. 79
Battiste, M. A. 111; *Decolonizing Education* 124; *Protecting Indigenous Knowledge and Heritage* 124
Belliveau, G. 98
Bennett, J. 29
Berg Press 80
Berry, W. 133
Bhabha, H. K. 94
Bickel, B. 57
Binder, M. J. 2, *58*, *59*, 66, 67
Bio-cultural Re-generation Institute 92
Blaikie, F. 2, 6, 15, 26–34, 27, *30*, *31*, *33*; affect theory 29; ancestral ways of knowing 30–32; City of Thunder Bay Millennium Award 28; Community Arts and Heritage Education Project (CAHEP) 28; disciplinary boundaries 28–29; engagements with community/ies 28; hermeneutic phenomenology 27–28; holistic pedagogy 32–33; new materialism 29; pedagogy 29–30; posthumanism 29; social-justice oriented research creation work 32

Index 161

Blair, A. 111, 113
Blood transfusions 86–87
Bobbit, J. 125
Bonhoeffer, D. 133
Booth, D. 2, 4, 60, 63; mentorship 59–62
Bourdieu, P. 34
Brandoni, L. 78
Brenneis, D.: "Doing Anthropology in Sound" 79
Bresler, L.: *Arts Education Policy Review* 79
Britzman, D. 142
Bull, M.: *The Auditory Culture Reader* 80

CACS *see* Canadian Association for Curriculum Studies (CACS)
CAHEP *see* Community Arts and Heritage Education Project (CAHEP) 28
Cajete, G.: *Look to the Mountain* 125
Canadian Association for Curriculum Studies (CACS) 12, 13, 106, 135, 141, 142, 144, 145
Canadian Curriculum Studies 10
Chambers, C. 12, 14, 52–54, 127, 141, 157
Cicero, M. 109
circularity 124
City of Thunder Bay's Arts and Heritage Committee 28
Clandinen, J. 80
Clandinin, J. 11, 12, 45, 148, 156, 157
Clarke, A. 42
Clark, J.: City of Thunder Bay Millennium Award 28
Cockburn, B. 138
Cohen, S.: *Steel Town Down* 147–152, *147, 152*
Cole, A. 12
Cole, P. 93
College of Teacher 9
Community Arts and Heritage Education Project (CAHEP) 28
complexity theory 133
Connelly, M. 3, 8, 11, 12, 45, 148, 156, 157
Conquergood, D. 89
Conrad, D. 13
constructivist theory 133
Coole, D. 29

Culleton, B. 142
Cunningham, S. 111
currere 37, 53, 148, 151, 156–157
curricular knowing, as spiritual praxis 69–76
curriculum 2–3, 53; adoption and 130–133; of care 77–81; as content 133; disruption of 45–49; derailed planning 47; living and working narratively 49; mentor of the same name 47–49; journey, picture-books-inspired 116–120; as meditative inquiry 41; as praxis 133; as process 133; soulful 73–74; studies 7–16, 145; theory 3, 14, 15, 43, 57, 69, 124, 125, 132, 149–150
Curriculum and Pedagogy Conference, University of Victoria (2001) 81
Curriculum Development and Performance Studies 84
Cuthbert, M. 111, 112

Davidson, J. 78
De Groot, J. 119
Dei, G. 113
Deleuze, G. 29
Denzin, N. 12
Derrida, J. 92, 93, 96
developmental theory 133
Dewey, J. 8, 71, 125, 149
dialogical meditative inquiry 41
Dillon, D. 142
Dimitiradis, G. 80, 81
Disruption Innovation Model 46
disruptive technology 46
Doll, W., Jr. 12, 52
Donald, D. 125, 126
Doolittle, E. 111, 112
Downey, A. M. 5, 123
Drake, S. 11, 22
Drobnick, J. 80
Dunlop, R. 32

ego 56
Eichler, M. 111, 113
elitist narcissism 83
Embodied Poetic Narrative 89
Engaging with Meditative Inquiry in Teaching, Learning, and Research: Realizing Transformative Potentials in Diverse Contexts 41–42
English Quarterly 142

162   *Index*

Eppert, C. 52, 55
Erickson, F. 80
Erlmann, V. 80
Ermine, W. 126
ethical relationality 126
ethical space 126

false-self-system 9
Feld, S. 78–79, 87; *Sound and Sentiment: Birds Weeping, Poetics, and Song in Kaluli Expression* 78
Fels, L. 84
5th Biennial Provoking Curriculum Conference, Edmonton (2011) 144
Figueroa, A. L. 78
final field trip 87–90
Fisher, L. 111
Fitznor, L. 111, 112
Floyd, G. 5, 131
forgiveness 25
Foucault, M. 108–109
Fredriksen, B. 79
Freire, P. 32, 111, 112
friendship 63–65
Frost, S. 29

Galarraga, M. L. 78
Galvin, K. 13
Gaztambide-Fernández, R. A. 123, 125
geo-metrons sounding 92–96
Gershon, W. S. 5, 77; *Sensuous Curriculum: Politics and the Senses in Education* 81; *Sound Curriculum: Sonic Studies in Educational Theory, Method, and Practice* 81
gifts 1–8, 15, 16, 23, 25, 45, 49, 57, 67, 87, 88, 90, 92–96, 98–104, 113, 118, 119, 120, 123–127, 133, 140; of being 149–150; curricular 148, 156–157; of friendship 63–65; and intellectual passion 105–109; of lingering in cultural legacy 154–158; of mentorship 59–62; (re)membering Indigenous curriculum theorists 123–127; *Steel Town Down* 147–152; of teaching 65–67; worlding 26–34
Glesne, C. 12
Goldman, I. 111
Gotan, M. C. 43
Gottleib, A. 79

grace 1–5, 7, 14, 15, 25, 49, 69–76; and intellectual passion 105–109; *Steel Town Down* 147–152; welcoming 92–96; worlding 33–34
Graham, P. 79
Grande, S. 95; *Red Pedagogy* 125
gratitude 1–5, 7, 8, 14, 23, 25, 26, 52, 56, 94–96, 110, 134–138; and curriculum disruption 45–49; definition of 134; for gifts of education 98–104; and intellectual passion 105–109; labyrinth of 57–67; narrative of 40–43; (re)membering Indigenous curriculum theorists 123–127; *Steel Town Down* 147–152; way of 37–43; words of 127; worlding 33–34
Graveline, F. J.: *Circle Works* 124–125
Greene, M. 8, 79
Gregg, M. 108
Grumet, M. 52–54, 127; *Toward a Poor Curriculum* 144
Guattari, F. 29
Guiney Yallop, J. J. 28, 32; curriculum studies 10–14; introduction 2, 3, 5–6; invitation to Narrative Inquiry 22; invitation to run a road race 22–25
Gurdjieff, G. 41

Hall, S. 111
Haraway, D. 106
He, M. F. 81
Heathcote, D. 86, 89
Hegel, G. W. F. 149
Heidegger, M. 149
Heilbrun, C. 8, 12
Helfenbein, R. 79
Hemmel, J. 88
Henderson, J. Y.: *Protecting Indigenous Knowledge and Heritage* 124
hermeneutic phenomenology 27–28
highlanders 143
Highway, T. 142
Hildebrandt, K. 111
Hillman, J. 138; *The Force of Character and the Lasting Life* 137; "Loving Language: A Poet's Vocation and Vision" 137
Hodgetts, A. B. 14

Index 163

Holguin, J. 85, 90
holistic pedagogy 32–33
Hoogland, C. 22
hooks, b. 8, 32, 157
Howes, D. 79–80
Huggan, I. 157–158
Husserl, E. 149

I Am Grateful 38–40
Imagination and Education
  Conference, Simon Fraser
  University (2004) 63
immanence 29
Indigenous Curriculum theorists, (re)
  membering 123–127
Indigenous Peoples Atlas of Canada
  14–15
individualization 16
Ingold, T. 157
inner life 143
inner-pre-service-self 9
INSEA *see* International Society
  for Education through Art
  (INSEA)
Institutionalized Racism in Higher
  Education 111
intellectual passion 105–109
intermingling souls 83–84
International Society for Education
  through Art (INSEA) 29
International Symposium on Poetic
  Inquiry (ISPI) 13–14, 22, 23
"In the Midst" 90
Irigaray, L. 73
Irwin, R. 10, 12, 80, 98
ISPI *see* International Symposium on
  Poetic Inquiry (ISPI)

Jackson., M. 78
JCACS *see Journal of the Canadian
  Association for Curriculum Studies*
  (JCACS)
Johnson, R. 111, 113
Jordon, N. A. 57
*The Journal of Curriculum
  Theorizing* 123
*Journal of the Canadian Association
  for Curriculum Studies* (JCACS)
  141–144
Joyce, W. 116
Jung, C. 10, 14, 16; *The
  Undiscovered Self* 9
Justice, D. H. 127

Kabir 41
Kalsi, A. 41
Karagiosis, N.: *Vulnerable sites and
  guises: Studies of adult symboliz-
  ing experiences in three venues of
  education* 144
Kelly, V. 126
Kim, J.-H. 80
King, T. 111, 142
Kirkness, V. 111, 112
Knowles, G. 12
Krishnamurti, J. 41
Kumar, A. 2, 37, 127

Laing, R. D. 10; *The Divided Self* 9
Lawrence, D. H. 108
Leacock, S. 108
Lea, G. W. 4, 98–104; *Homa Bay
  Memories: Using Research-based
  Theatre to Explore a Narrative
  Inheritance* 98
Leggo, C. 4, 10, 12–14, 23, 32, 74,
  98, 108, 127, 134
Lessmore, M. 116
Lester 87, 88
Lewis, R. 111
Lincoln, Y. S. 12
Linton, J. 111
Lloyd, R. 61
Luce-Kapler, R. 144

Mabit, J. 95
MacGregor, R. 28
MacKenzie-Dawson, S. 3, 69
Mann, H. 125
Mantas, K. 2
*The Many Faces of Love: Celebrating
  the Lifework of Carl Leggo* (CACS
  2019 pre-conference) 135
Maracle, L. 142
Martin, B. 31
Mathew, R. 42
McGregor, D. 111, 112
McGregor, E. L. 111
McKay, A. 111, 112
McNiff, S. 12
Menon, S. 42
mentorship 59–62
Merriam, S. 12
Meyer, K. 42
Mignolo, W. 95
Milgram, S.: *Obedience to Authority*
  9–10

164 *Index*

Miller, J. L. 73–74, 141
Miller, J. P. 32
Minh-ha, T. T. 94
Miro, J. A. 78
Mitchell, C. 142, 143, 145
Mitchell, R. 78
Mojumdar, K. K. 42
Monague, J. 14
Montessori, M. 32
Moses, D. D. 142
multi-faceted legacy of place 157–158
Mundi, A. 92
music, as meditative inquiry 41

Nachmanovitch, S. 65
Narrative Inquiry 11
Narrative Inquiry Self-Study 10
National Indian Brotherhood: *Indian Control of Indian Education* 141
Neill, A. S. 32
Nellis, R. 4, 134
Nespor, J. 79
Newman, K. 148
new materialism 29
Ng-a-Fook, N. 13, 144
Noblit, G. 81
Nochlin, L. 29
Noddings, N. 32
Norris, J.: *What do scholars want?*, 107

Oberg, A. 52, 54
O'Donoghue, D. 29
Ontario College of Teachers 9
Ontario Institute for Studies in Education 113
ontological insecurity 9
O'Riley, P. 93
Orwell, G. 134
Osho 41

Palmer, P. J. 12, 49, 57
Palulis, P. 6, 92
Parr, K. 111
pedagogy 29–30, 93; holistic 32–33; Indigenous critical 125; linking the past with the future, Indigenous influences on 110–115; pedagogical resonances 77–81; posthuman 30, 31
Performative Inquiry 89
Phelan, A. 42

picturebooks-inspired curriculum journey 116–120
Pinar, W. F. 2, 4, 8, 12, 14, 15, 37, 42, 47, 52, 55, 61, 69, 72, 81, 127, 148, 150, 156; *Autobiography, politics and sexuality: Essays in curriculum theory 1972–1992* 10; *Toward a Poor Curriculum* 144; *Towards a Poor Curriculum* 53
Pitawanakwat, L. 111
Podolski, A. G. 147, *147*; curriculum studies 8–10, 14–16; introduction 2–5, 7
polyphonic pathology 78–81
Portelli, J. P. 119
posthumanism 29
Powell, K. 79
Prendergast, M. 13, 22
Price, R.: *Two Evenings in Saramaka* 78
Price, S.: *Two Evenings in Saramaka* 78
Provoking Curriculum conference 53, 55

Qualitative Inquiry 54
Quesnelle, R. 14

Radford, L. 141–143, 145
Restoule, J.-P. 5, 110
Rice, K. 111, 112
Ricketts, K. 6, 83, *90*
Rilke, R. M. 73
Rintoul, H. 2
Robertson, J. 141
Rosiek, J. 80
Ross, E. W. 42–43
Roy, B. 78
Ruitenberg, C. 96

Sachamama Biocultural Regeneration Institute 93
SAGE *see* Supporting Aboriginal Graduate Enhancement (SAGE)
Sameshima, P. 12, 13
Scheffel, T.-L. 5, 116, *117*
Schlamb, C. 2, 45
scholarship, as narrative research-creation 32–33
Schubert, B. 81
Sebald, W. G. 56; *A Place in the Country* 52
Seigel, M. 86

Index   165

Seigworth, G. 108
self-in-relation 125
serendipity 2, 8, 15, 52–56, 154, 158
Sharma, K. K. 42
Shields, C. 22, 32, 48, 150, 154; curriculum studies 8, 10–13; introduction 2–4, 6–7
Silicon Valley (HBO) 46
Sinner, A. 4, 13, 105
Smith, D. 111
Smith, G. 111, 113
Smith, L. 111
social-justice oriented research creation work 32
Special Interest Group 13
Spector, H. 43
Spindler, G. 79
Steele, B. 63–65, *64*; *Draw Me a Story* 63
Steel Town Down 147–152, *147, 152*
Steiner, R. 32
Sterne, J. 80
Stewart, K. 34
Stogan, V. 110
Stoller, P.: *Sensuous Scholarship* 79; *Taste of Ethnographic Things: The Senses in Anthropology* 79
Storying the World 108
Strong-Wilson, T. 2, 52, 144, 145; *Provoking curriculum encounters across educational experience (Studies in Curriculum Theory Series)* 15
Styres, S. 124
Sumara, D. 144
Summerhill 32
Supporting Aboriginal Graduate Enhancement (SAGE) 113
synchronicity 143

tacit wisdom 150
Taylor, D. H. 142
teaching: gift of 65–67; as meditative inquiry 41–42
Ted T. Aoki Award for Distinguished Service within the Field of Canadian Curriculum Studies 141
theory of BIGNESS 87
Tippet, K. 69–70
Tisdell, E. 12
Tuck, E. 123, 125
Tyler, R. 8

un-embodied-self 9

Vaandering, D. 6, 130
van Manen, M. 27, 32
Varese, S. 92–93, 95
Venkatarman, V. R. 78
Vibert, A. B. 119
Vonnegut, K. 111, 114
Vyas, V. 43

Walpole, H. 52
Weber, S. 142, 143
Weiss, M. 78
welcoming grace 93, 95–96
Whittaker, E. 94–95
Who Am I?, 40
Williams, J. B. 78
Windsor Communication Studies 111
Wong, D. 79
working against replacement 123–124
Wozolek, B. 77

Yoder, A. 52, 55–56

Zwicky, J. 157